Contents

How to use this book

Designed to complement the Book 2 textbook, the contents of this revision guide will help you prepare you for your final exams.

This revision guide covers:

- Eduqas AS Level components 1 and 2
- Eduqas A Level components 1, 2 and 3
- WJEC AS Level units 1 and 2
- WJEC A Level units 3 and 4.

There is also a selection of learning features throughout the topics:

Spec spotlight: mapping of each topic to the relevant specifications for easy navigation

Link: references back to the Book 1 textbook to refresh your topic knowledge in more depth

Revision booster: ideas and suggestions to help you revise more effectively and help you achieve the higher marks

Build your revision notes around: a concise recap of pertinent information you should ensure you know in each topic

Activity: a variety of activities to apply your knowledge and develop your understanding

Quickfire questions: at the end of each topic to test knowledge and understanding.

AS/A Level qualifications

This revision guide is intended to support the A Level study of both Eduqas and WJEC. Additional content required for AS and some A Level specifications for both Eduqas and WJEC can be found in the Revision Guide Book 1 (ISBN 978 1 912820 10 8).

The content coverage section opposite explains exactly what can be found in each book. References to the WJEC specifications are represented by the letter **W** and references to the Eduqas specifications are represented by the letter **E**. Content that is only relevant to specific parts of the Eduqas specifications is colour coded in both the main text and the topic overview tables in each chapter.

EDUQAS A-LEVEL

Eduqas A Level only (blue)

Book 1 Revision Guide	Book 2 Revision Guide
Law making, the nature of law and the Welsh and English legal systems **E1.1.1 W1.1** Law making Law reform **E1.1.2 W1.2** Delegated legislation **E1.1.3 W1.3** Statutory interpretation **E1.1.4 W1.4** Judicial precedent **E1.2.1 W1.5** Civil courts **E1.2.2 W1.6** Criminal process Juries **E1.2.3 W1.7** Legal personnel: Barristers and solicitors Judiciary Magistrates **E1.2.4 W1.8** Access to justice and funding **Law of contract** **E2.1.1 W3.6** Rules of contract **E2.1.2 W3.7** Essential requirements of a contract **E2.1.3 E2.1.5 W3.10** Discharge of contract **E2.1.4 E2.1.6 W3.11** Remedies: Contract **Law of tort** **E2.2.1 W2.1** Rules of tort **E2.2.2 W2.2** Liability in negligence **E2.2.3 W2.3** Occupier's liability **E2.2.4 E2.2.7 W2.**4 Remedies: Tort **Criminal law** **E2.3.2 W3.13** General elements of criminal liability **E2.3.3 W3.14** Offences against the person **Human rights law** **E2.4.1 E 2.4.2 W3.1** Rules, theory and protection of human rights law **E2.4.3 W3.2** Specific provisions of the ECHR **E2.4.5 E2.4.6 W3.5** Reform of human rights **E2.4.4 W3.3** Restrictions of the ECHR	**Law of contract** **E2.1.3 W3.8** Express and implied terms **E2.1.4 W3.9** Misrepresentation and economic duress **Law of tort** **E2.2.4** Torts connected to land **E2.2.5** Vicarious liability **E2.2.6** Defences: Tort **Criminal law** **E2.3.3 W3.14** Fatal offences against the person **E2.3.4 W3.15** Property offences **E2.3.5 E2.3.6 W3.16 W3.17** Capacity and necessity defences

Which qualification are you studying for?

You may be studying for either Eduqas qualifications or WJEC qualifications. This revision guide covers the examination requirements for both. Most of the content is very similar in all the specifications, and the questions and mark schemes differ only slightly.

For more information, look at the examination guidance section of the Book 2 textbook and the examination papers and mark schemes of the qualification for which you are studying and discuss them with your teacher.

WJEC AS/A Level examination content: Wales

In Wales, most candidates will be studying for the WJEC AS in their first year, followed by the A Level in their second year. In most cases, AS exams will be sat at the end of the first year and these will be combined with the A Level exams, which are sat at the end of the second year, to achieve the full A Level qualification. For the full WJEC specification content, go to www.wjec.co.uk.

The AS is less challenging and worth 40% of the full A Level qualification.

The AS is a stepping stone to the full A Level, so ideas introduced at AS will be developed on the full A Level papers.

A full WJEC A Level has four units or examinations. This content is covered across both Revision Guide Books 1 and 2.

A WJEC AS Level has two units or examinations. This revision guide includes enough topics to help you prepare for the exams.

<table>
<tr><th></th><th>Unit 1</th><th>Unit 2</th><th>Unit 3</th><th>Unit 4</th></tr>
<tr><td rowspan="3">WJEC AS Level</td><td>The nature of law and the Welsh and English legal systems</td><td>The law of tort</td><td>n/a</td><td>n/a</td></tr>
<tr><td>80 marks available (25% of full A Level qualification)</td><td>60 marks available (15% of full A Level qualification)</td><td>n/a</td><td>n/a</td></tr>
<tr><td>1 hour and 45 minutes</td><td>1 hour and 30 minutes</td><td>n/a</td><td>n/a</td></tr>
<tr><td rowspan="3">WJEC A Level</td><td colspan="2" rowspan="3">Units 1 and 2, above, plus units 3 and 4
100 marks available (30% of full A Level qualification)
1 hour and 45 minutes</td><td>The practice of substantive law</td><td>Substantive law perspectives</td></tr>
<tr><td>100 marks available (30% of full A Level qualification)</td><td>100 marks available (30% of full A Level qualification)</td></tr>
<tr><td>2 hours</td><td>2 hours</td></tr>
</table>

The overall weightings are 40% for AS and 60% for A Level.

- **Unit 1**: The nature of law and the Welsh and English legal systems (25%).
- **Unit 2**: The law of tort (15%).
- **Unit 3**: The practice of substantive law (30%).
- **Unit 4**: Substantive law perspectives (30%).

In England, most candidates will be studying for the Eduqas AS or A Level. For the full Eduqas specification content, go to www.eduqas.co.uk.

The Eduqas AS Level is half of the content of the full A Level but is as equally challenging as the full A Level.

A full Eduqas A Level has three components or examinations. This content is covered over both Revision Guide Books 1 and 2.

A full Eduqas AS Level has two components or examinations. This revision guide includes enough topics to help you prepare for the exams.

	Component 1	Component 2	Component 3
Eduqas AS Level	The nature of law and the English legal system	Understanding substantive law	n/a
	60 marks available (50% of qualification)	60 marks available (50% of qualification)	n/a
	1 hour and 30 minutes	1 hour and 30 minutes	n/a
Eduqas A Level	The nature of law and the English legal system	Substantive law in practice	Perspectives of substantive law
	50 marks available (25% of qualification)	75 marks available (37.5% of qualification)	75 marks available (37.5% of qualification)
	1 hour and 30 minutes	2 hours and 15 minutes	2 hours and 15 minutes

AS Level Law with Eduqas is a stand-alone qualification and is weighted at 40% of the overall A Level. Each component is worth 50% of the qualification.

A Level Law with Eduqas is a linear course and the components are weighted as follows:

- **Component 1**: 25%.
- **Component 2**: 37.5%.
- **Component 3**: 37.5%.

Here is some guidance on how you can apply, analyse and evaluate your knowledge when answering questions on different aspects of law.

AO2: Apply questions

I: Identify the area of law concerned

- Introduce the topic.
- Define key terms in the question.
- Identify key points – for example, what is the area of law?
- Who is the defendant? Who is the claimant?

Take care to avoid a waffly introduction – directly address the topic concerned from your very first sentence.

D: Describe the area of law concerned

- Explain the area of law, and use supporting legal authority to help your explanation.
- You do not need to know the years of cases, only statutes.
- It is good practice to underline legal authority if you have time.

There is no need for detailed facts of cases – a short explanation as to why it is relevant is enough, unless there are significant similarities between the case you are citing and the facts in the problem scenario.

A: Apply the law to the scenario

- Apply the **D** to the parties in the scenario – what is the outcome?
- You can explore more than one possibility.
- Mention the parties' names as often as you can.
- Refer to **everything** in the scenario.

AO3: Analyse and evaluate questions

Certain words and phrases help you to form a logical argument, and show that you have carefully considered all the relevant points and issues. Some examples are in the tables below.

Beginning to build points and sequence ideas

Start your answer by explaining the key points and the main legal ideas.

Building points in sequence	Adding to points	Using tentative language	Illustrating a point or idea
Firstly, Secondly, Thirdly etc ...	One point might be ...	It could be argued that ...	I think that ... For example ...
To begin, it can be said ...	In addition, ...	One possibility would be ...	There are lots of reasons that ..., such as ...
The next point would be ...	Moreover, ...	It might be said that ...	You could argue that ... For instance ...
To take this further, it can be said ...	Also, ...	Some would say ...	One example of ... would be ...
Furthermore ...	Additionally ...	I would suggest ...	The idea that ... is supported by ...
Finally, ...	Next, ...	Maybe it's fair to argue that ...	

Making stronger, more forceful points and arguments

Make sure you justify what you are saying. This is where key legal authority, current affairs and reforms can be included.

Using interrogative phrases (useful for reforms)	Justifying ideas (useful for reforms)	Emphasising points	Starting with adverbs
Might it not be suggested that ...	The [case] tells us that.... therefore....	Above all, it must be said that ...	Interestingly, ...
Could it be said that....	The [recent article] says ... Thus, ...	It is particularly true that ...	Undeniably,...
Might we not argue that...	The [recent reforms] ... so ...	Most significantly, ...	Clearly, ...
Is it fair to conclude that...	It can be seen that [statistics, legal authority] ... consequently ...	Most notable is the fact that ...	Evidently, ...
Might it be true that ...		It is particularly important to highlight that ...	Certainly, ...
			Really, ...
			Obviously, ...
			Undoubtedly, ...
			Surely, ...

Making balanced, considered points and arguments

This is where you will link your points and refer back to the question. Use legal authority and supporting theorists where you can.

Comparing	Contrasting	Presenting a balanced discussion
Similarly, I think that ...	Unlike ..., it can be said that ...	On the one hand, you could say ... but, on the other hand, you could also argue ...
Likewise, it is my opinion that ...	Alternatively, it can be said that ...	One argument would be ... but another point of view would be ...
I think that, in the same way, it could be said that ...	In contrast, it can be argued that ...	It might be said that ...; however, it might also be said that ...
Equally, it could be argued that ...	Whereas many people think that ..., it is my opinion that ...	One might think that ... but conversely it could also be argued that ...
Like ..., it is true to say that ...	You could say ... but I think that ...	One line of thought is .... Alternatively, another opinion would be ...

Assessment in Eduqas and WJEC Law

As you begin your revision, it will help you to remind yourself of the Assessment Objectives that you are being tested on. These consist of the following:

- **Assessment Objective 1 (AO1)**: Describing what you know.
- **Assessment Objective 2 (AO2)**: Applying your knowledge.
- **Assessment Objective 3 (AO3)**: Analysing/evaluating this knowledge.

All mark schemes offer marks for the different skills and examiners are trained to look for and recognise them.

- **AO1**: You must demonstrate knowledge and understanding of legal rules and principles.
- **AO2**: You must apply legal rules and principles to given scenarios in order to present a legal argument using appropriate legal terminology.
- **AO3**: You must analyse and evaluate legal rules, principles, concepts and issues.

Key terms and legal authority

Students often say that studying law is like learning a whole new language. In fact, you will need to become familiar with some Latin terms, such as *ratio decidendi*. If you are to get into the top mark bands, you need to use appropriate legal terminology. Key terms are highlighted throughout the book. Many of the shorter exam questions will require you to explain the meaning of a term or describe a concept. Extended-response essays should always start with an explanation of the key term in the question. The rest of your answer should focus on ideas and debates related to that key term.

In order to support the points you make, you should include legal authority. This can be a case, statute or legislation, for example ***Rylands v Fletcher (1866)*** or ***s1 Theft Act 1968***.

CHAPTER 1 THE LAW OF CONTRACT

Express and implied terms of a contract

Spec spotlight

WJEC A Level
3.8: Express and implied terms, conditions, warranties and innominate terms, exclusion and limitation clauses

Eduqas A Level
2.1.3: Express and implied terms

In this section students will develop their knowledge of:

- Obligations under a contract: difference between representations and terms
- Express terms: incorporation of express terms, parole and evidence rule
- Implied terms: terms implied by fact, terms implied by statute: implied terms under the ***Consumer Rights Act 2015***. ***Consumer Contract Regulations 2013***
- Exclusion clauses in both consumer and business-to-business contracts: incorporation of exclusion clauses, ***Unfair Contract Terms Act 1977***
- Other terms: conditions, warranties, innominate terms

LINK

For more on express and implied terms, see pages 8–20 of *WJEC/Eduqas A Level Law Book 2*.

Revision booster

There could be questions on this topic covering all three assessment objectives.

For **AO2** questions, you need to **apply** whether the terms in a problem scenario have been lawfully incorporated. You should include cases to support each element of law and, as **AO2** is the skill being tested, it is essential to apply the law to the scenario provided. Using the **IDA** structure is helpful for these types of questions:

- **Introduction**: identify the legal issue concerned and define any key terms that are central to the topic.
- **Description**: describe the area of law, using legal authority, supporting cases and/or statute provisions.
- **Application**: This is the crucial element of the answer. You should refer to the names of the people in the scenario, and use phrases such as 'In this case…'.

For **AO3 evaluation** questions, you need to analyse and evaluate an area of the law. Elements of this topic that could feature as an evaluation question include the effectiveness of the legislation that incorporates terms by statute, as well as an evaluation of the fairness of exclusion clauses. As evaluation is the skill being tested, it is important to include an introduction, a paragraphed main body that links back to the question, and a conclusion to support your argument, including as much legal authority as you can, with reference to reforms where appropriate.

Build your revision notes around...

- **Express terms**
  - Incorporated by:
    - being written into the contract, or
    - making a statement prior to the contract's conclusion
  - Guidelines on incorporation:
    - Importance of statement: ***Bannerman v White (1861)***
    - Knowledge and skill of the person making the statement: ***Dick Bentley Productions v Harold Smith Motors (1965)***
    - The timing of the statement: ***Routledge v McKay (1954)***
- **Implied terms: by fact**
  - ***Marks and Spencer v BNP Paribas (2015)***
  - To be implied by fact:
    - without the term, the contract would lack commercial or practical coherence
    - term must be necessary for business efficacy: ***The Moorcock (1889)***
    - term must satisfy the **business necessity test** (previously known as the **officious bystander test**): ***Shirlaw v Southern Foundries (1926)***
- **Implied terms: by law**
  - Sale of goods: ***Consumer Rights Act 2015***:
    - ***s9***: satisfactory quality
    - ***s10***: fit for purpose
    - ***s11***: as described
  - Supply of services: ***Consumer Rights Act 2015***:
    - ***s49***: reasonable care and skill
    - ***s50***: binding information
    - ***s51***: reasonable price
    - ***s52***: reasonable time

- **Unfair terms: in law**
  - ***s62 Consumer Rights Act 2015:*** any term that is unfair under the Act is not binding
  - A term is unfair if it is contrary to the requirement of good faith; it causes a significant imbalance in the parties' rights and obligations
  - ***Consumer Contracts (Information, Cancellation and Additional Charges) Regulations 2013***: outlines key information that should be provided to consumers entering into contracts online, by phone or from a catalogue
    - Consumer has the right to cancel within 14 days after ordering
- **Exclusion clauses: common law**
  - Must be incorporated:
    - by signature: ***L'Estrange v Graucob (1934)***
    - by reasonable notice: ***Parker v South Eastern Railway (1877)***
    - by a previous course of dealing: ***Spurling v Bradshaw (1956)***
  - Exclusion clause has to cover the breach

- **Exclusion clauses: statute**
  - ***Unfair Contract Terms Act 1977*** applies only to non-consumer contracts
    - ***s2***: exclusion of liability for negligence
    - ***s3***: exclusion of liability for breach of contract
    - ***s6***: exclusion of liability in contracts for sale of goods
    - ***s11***: reasonableness test

Activity 1.1 Legal authority

Match the relevant section of ***Consumer Rights Act 2015*** to the rule it outlines.

Legal authority	Rule
s9	Services must be provided at a reasonable price.
s10	An unfair term is not binding on the consumer.
s11	The consumer's legal right to reject goods that are of unsatisfactory quality.
s20	Goods must be fit for purpose.
s23	Goods must be of satisfactory quality.
s49	If a service does not satisfy criteria, trader should redo the inadequate element at no extra cost.
s50	Where repeat performance of the service is not possible, the consumer can obtain a price reduction.
s51	Goods must be as described.
s52	Retailer must be given the opportunity to repair or replace defective goods outside the 30 days of purchase.
s55	Services must be undertaken with reasonable care and skill.
s56	Any information given to the consumer before the service is provided is binding.
s62	Services must be provided within a reasonable time.

Activity 1.2 Implied terms

Look at the following scenarios and discuss your rights as a consumer in relation to the terms contained in the contract. You will need to look at relevant sections of the ***Consumer Rights Act 2015*** and the ***Consumer Contracts (Information, Cancellation and Additional Charges) Regulations 2013***.

Continued

What are your consumer rights?

a. You buy a laptop and use it frequently for four months. Then, you notice that the battery is not performing properly and the charge is only lasting an hour. The trader performs a repair but the laptop continues to be slow and runs out of charge quickly.

b. You buy a new coffee pod machine but after a week you notice that the milk is spitting everywhere, so the coffee machine is not of satisfactory quality.

c. You are planning to do some home maintenance and are looking to buy a new power drill. You have a particular model in mind and discuss the requirements with the salesperson, including the need to drill masonry. The salesperson agrees that the drill and its bits are suitable for the task. However, when you try to drill a wall using the new drill, you find that it is not suitable for masonry.

d. You download a free game which involves building a virtual world. You earn some virtual currency by playing the game and you then make an in-app purchase of some additional virtual currency, which costs you £3.99. However, the currency does not appear in your virtual world.

e. A TV series download is described as containing all 13 episodes of a season. After you have paid to download it, you find that the final episode is missing.

Continued

f. You buy an app for organising music and photos but, when you start to use it, a bug causes it to delete your music and photos.

g. You contract with a catering service to provide a buffet for your birthday party at 6 pm on a specified Saturday. You pay £25 per head for the service. A clause in the contract states that the maximum discount for any service problem caused by the supplier is £70. However, the buffet is delivered late, at 10 pm, as the party is ending.

h. You contract a trader to decorate a room for a party. You inspect the work the day before it is due to be finished but it is not the colour scheme you agreed with the trader's assistant. The trader phones the assistant, who agrees that you did specify the colour scheme.

i. You sign up to a mobile phone contract for £20 a month. The day after you agree to the deal, you discover that your neighbour has got the same package for £15 a month. You challenge the firm, arguing that its deal is unfair.

j. You purchase a plane ticket from SoarPrice Airlines and see a phrase on the last booking screen stating that 'extra fees may apply'. You tick the box next to it and book your ticket. When you arrive at the airport, you find that you have to pay an excess baggage fee.

Activity 1.3 Application question (*taken from WJEC/Eduqas SAMs material*)

You may need to apply the essential requirements of a contract to a scenario in order to advise someone on whether their terms have been incorporated and are fair. With questions like this, it is suggested that you take each event in chronological order and follow the IDA structure is followed (see page xx).

1. Florence bought a new TV aerial from TVs R Us. The salesperson assured her that it would improve the quality of her television reception. Florence arranged for Jamie to install the aerial. Jamal missed two appointments, for which Florence had taken time off work. When he finally turned up, he dropped his tools while installing the aerial and damaged four roof tiles. Though the aerial was properly installed, it was of poor quality and failed to improve the television reception.

   TVs R Us refused to accept any responsibility.

   Jamie pointed out that Florence had signed a completion of work form, which included a statement that he would not be liable for any damage resulting from the installation work.

Applying your knowledge of legal rules and principles, advise Florence on whether there has been a breach of any implied or express terms for the purchase and installation of the aerial.

2. Fiona bought a battery powerpack because the battery on her mobile phone did not last longer than a day. The purchase included access to a website from which she could download an app that promised to extend her phone's battery life by eight hours. However, the app corrupted her phone's operating system, and she lost all the photographs and videos on her phone. In addition, the casing on the battery powerpack became loose and hot when in use. After two weeks, she complained to Saira, the owner of Batteries 4 Life, where she had bought the powerpack. Saira referred Fiona to clauses in the contract of supply that claimed to restrict the trader's liability to the purchase price of the goods for breach of satisfactory quality. The contract then stated that, that subject to this, there was 'no liability whatsoever' for any other breach.

Applying your knowledge of legal rules and principles, advise Fiona on whether she is entitled to recover the losses incurred.

Context

Remember the three ways in which exclusion clauses can be incorporated under the common law.

- **By signature**: if a document is signed at the time of the contract, its contents become the terms of that contract, regardless of whether the consumer has read the terms.
- **By reasonable notice**: if a party gives separate terms at the time the contract is made, those terms become part of the contract if the consumer has had reasonable notice that they exist.
- **By a previous course of dealing**: if two parties have previously made contracts with each other, it is assumed that the same exclusion clauses apply to subsequent transactions.

Activity 1.4 Exclusion clauses

Consider whether the following exclusion clauses have been successfully incorporated. Give reasons for your answer and support it with legal authority where appropriate.

Example	Exclusion clause successfully implemented? (Yes/No)	Reason and case example(s)
1. A notice placed on the counter in a shop.		
2. A notice in a signed contract.		
3. A notice contained in a delivery note where the parties have regularly dealt on the same terms.		
4. A notice placed on a hotel bedroom wall.		
5. A notice contained in a receipt.		
6. A notice on the back of a cloakroom ticket.		
7. A notice posted on the machine at the entrance to a car park.		

Context

Research the Law Commission's report *Unfair Terms in Contracts (LC No 298)* and have a look at the Draft Bill proposed in it. This will help you evaluate this area of law and look at ways in which the statutory controls on exclusion clauses could be improved.

Activity 1.5 Importance of terms

Term	Explanation	Supporting case(s)
Conditions	Terms that cannot be identified until the contract has been breached.	*Hong Kong Fir v Kawasaki (1962)*
Warranties	Major terms of a contract. So important that a failure to perform would render the contract meaningless.	*Poussard v Spiers & Pond (1976)*
Innominate terms	Minor term of a contract. A breach means the party can sue for damages but not reject the contract.	*Bettini v Gye (1876)*

Using the relevant coloured highlighter, highlight in the following statement which terms are the conditions, warranties and innominate terms.

I arrange for Jack to mow my lawn every Tuesday morning for £20 per week. This Tuesday evening, I am hosting a barbecue for my friends so I need the garden to look well kept.

1.1 Quickfire questions

1. Explain the difference between **representations** and **terms**.
2. Outline the **three** ways in which an express term can be incorporated into a contract.
3. Why is the literal interpretation the preferred method of interpretation for contracts?
4. What is the significance of ***Marks and Spencer v BNP Paribas (2015)***?
5. What redress is available for consumers who are bringing a claim for defective **goods** under the ***Consumer Rights Act 2015***?
6. What redress is available for consumers who are bringing a claim for **unsatisfactory services** provided under the ***Consumer Rights Act 2015***?
7. Outline **three** key pieces of information that must be provided to a consumer under the ***Consumer Contracts (Information, Cancellation and Additional Charges) Regulations 2013***.
8. Under the ***Consumer Contracts (Information, Cancellation and Additional Charges) Regulations 2013***, what rights does a consumer have to cancel their purchase after 14 days?
9. Outline the **three** ways in which an exclusion clause can be incorporated into a contract.
10. What is the purpose of the ***Unfair Contract Terms Act 1977***?
11. What is meant by a **warranty**?

Misrepresentation and economic duress

Spec Spotlight	In this section students will develop their knowledge of:
WJEC A Level **3.9:** Misrepresentation and economic duress **Eduqas A Level** **2.1.4:** Misrepresentation and economic duress	• Fraudulent misrepresentation: the meaning of fraudulent misrepresentation and the remedies available • Innocent misrepresentation: the meaning of innocent misrepresentation and the remedies available • Negligent misrepresentation: the meaning of negligent representation and the remedies available • ***Misrepresentation Act 1967***: statutory misrepresentation under ***s2***, the limitation of liability under ***s3*** and the remedies available • Economic duress: meaning of economic duress, distinction from duress to the person and any available remedies

LINK

For more on misrepresentation and economic duress, see pages 21–25 of *WJEC/ Eduqas A Level Law Book 2*.

Revision booster

This topic could feature as a scenario-type question testing **AO2 application** skills. For this type of question, you need to advise someone on the issues. You would normally use the facts of the scenario to decide whether there has been misrepresentation, the type of misrepresentation and the remedies available. This type of scenario question could also ask you to consider an application of the rules on economic duress and the remedies available. For these longer responses, you should also structure your answer using an introduction that provides an overview of misrepresentation and economic duress and a conclusion that ties together the issues and reaches a conclusion based on your application. As **AO2** is the skill being tested, you must apply the law to the scenario provided, using cases and statutes to support your answer.

This topic could also feature as an essay question testing **AO3 analysis and evaluation** skills. Think about the elements of each topic that could warrant a higher mark, more evaluative response. Some possible questions might be as follows:

- To what extent does the ***Misrepresentation Act 1967*** protect buyers against negligent statements made by sellers?
- Does the law of misrepresentation provide adequate remedies for consumers?
- Analyse and evaluate the law in respect of misrepresentation and economic duress.

For these longer responses, you should start your answer with an introduction that provides an overview of what you will discuss and how the main body will progress. It could also provide some brief context, along with an explanation of key terms in relation to the topic or question. Your answer should then follow a logical paragraphed structure with a link back to the question and use evidence to support it. A conclusion should tie together the issues based on the evidence you have presented and in relation to the question. In order to evaluate, you also need to explain what it is you are evaluating.

Build your revision notes around...

- **Misrepresentation:**
  - A false statement in a contract that can cause the contract to be voidable
  - A statement of material fact, made by one party to a contract to the other party, during the negotiations leading up to the formation of the contract, which was intended to, and did, operate as an inducement under the contract, and which was untrue or incorrectly stated
- **Fraudulent misrepresentation**: fraud must be proved: ***Derry v Peak (1889)*** but overruled by the ***Companies Act 2006***
  - Remedies: damages according to tort and the ***Misrepresentation Act 1967*** and rescission
- **Negligent misrepresentation**: the principle in ***Hedley Byrne v Heller & Partners (1964)***
  - Three requirements: knowledge, proximity, reliance
  - Remedies: damages according to tort measure of negligence and the ***Misrepresentation Act 1967***
- **Innocent misrepresentation**: ***Misrepresentation Act 1967***: only claims where a party believes their untrue statements to be true.
  - Remedies: rescission and damages under the ***Misrepresentation Act 1967***
- **Misrepresentation under statute**: ***s2(1) Misrepresentation Act 1967***
  - No need to prove fraud or special relationship under the ***Hedley Byrne*** criteria
  - Person making the statement must prove they were not negligent: ***Howard Marine and Dredging Co Ltd v A Ogden and Sons Ltd (1978)***, ***Spice Girls Ltd v Aprilla World Service (2002)***
- **Economic duress**: a contract may be set aside because extreme coercion has rendered the contract commercially unviable
  - **Five** conditions need to be satisfied:
    - Pressure was exerted on the contracting party: ***North Ocean Shipping Co v Hyundai Construction Co (1979) [The Atlantic Baron]***
    - Pressure was illegitimate: ***Atlas Express Ltd v Kafco (Importers and Distributors) Ltd (1989)***
    - Pressure induced the claimant to enter the contract: ***Barton v Armstrong (1975)***
    - Claimant had no choice but to enter the contract: ***Universe Tankships v International Transport Workers' Federation (1983)***
    - Claimant protested at the time or shortly after the contract was made: ***North Ocean Shipping Co v Hyundai Construction Co (1979) [The Atlantic Baron]***

Activity 1.6 What is misrepresentation?

Cases to use

Attwood v Small (1838)

Bisset v Wilkinson (1927)

Couchman v Hill (1947)

Edgington v Fitzmaurice (1885)

JEB Fasteners Ltd v Marks Bloom & Co Ltd (1983)

Peyman v Lanjani (1985)

Roscorla v Thomas (1842)

Select the cases from the list to show which ones influence which part of the definition of misrepresentation. Some parts of the definition have more than one case relating to them.

Misrepresentation is ...	Case examples
... a statement of material fact ...	
... made by one party to a contract to the other party ...	
... during the negotiations leading up to the formation of the contract ...	
... which was intended to operate and did operate as an inducement ...	
... under the contract, and which was untrue or incorrectly stated.	

Fraudulent misrepresentation

Where fraudulent misrepresentation is alleged, fraud must also be proved. ***Derry v Peak (1889)*** showed that, if a person makes a false statement that they do not believe to be true at the time, this is a fraudulent misrepresentation. The claimant will then sue for damages, which will be awarded according to the tort of deceit and are also available under ***s2(1) Misrepresentation Act 1967***. The equitable remedy of rescission is also available. The defendant is responsible for all losses, including any consequential loss that has a causal link between the fraudulent misrepresentation and the claimant's loss.

Negligent misrepresentation

According to ***Hedley Byrne v Heller & Partners (1964)***, damages may be recovered for a negligent misrepresentation where a financial loss has been incurred and where there is a special relationship between the parties.

There are three requirements:

1. The party making the statement must possess the particular type of knowledge for which the advice is required.

2. There must be sufficient proximity between the two parties that it is reasonable to rely on the statement.
3. The party to whom the statement is made relies on the statement and the party making the statement is aware of that reliance.

Damages are available under the ***Misrepresentation Act 1967***. The equitable remedy of rescission is also available.

Innocent misrepresentation

Any misrepresentation not made fraudulently was historically classed as an innocent misrepresentation, regardless of how it was made. Since the emergence of the ***Hedley Byrne*** principle and the passing of the ***Misrepresentation Act 1967***, the only misrepresentations that can be claimed to be made innocently are those where a party makes a statement with an honest belief in its truth. An example is where the party merely repeats inaccurate information, but is unaware that it is untrue.

The main remedy for innocent misrepresentation is the equitable remedy of rescission; that is, to void the contract as if it never happened. Damages are also available under ***s2(1) Misrepresentation Act 1967***.

Activity 1.7 Types of misrepresentation

What type of misrepresentation is involved in the following examples?

1. Jane is selling her sports car to Anna. Anna asks what capacity the engine is. Jane, after looking at the registration documents, tells her that it is a 1000cc. Jane does not know that the documents are incorrect.

   Type of misrepresentation:

2. Simon, a carpet salesperson, tells Ayesha that a rug can be cleaned with bleach, without checking the manufacturer's specification, which states that it cannot.

   Type of misrepresentation:

3. Emily, who has no qualifications at all, tells prospective employers at an interview that she has a degree in psychology.

   Type of misrepresentation:

4. Louise recently purchased 'beefburgers' from her local supermarket, but later read in the newspaper that the brand actually contained horsemeat.

   Type of misrepresentation:

Activity 1.8 Mead v Babington (2007)

Read the following case study and answer the questions that follow.

A couple wanted to build a property in Spain and made enquiries to a British estate agent. The estate agent introduced them to a Spanish developer with whom they arranged to have a property built. However, the property was not built and they lost a lot of money.

During negotiations, the estate agent had made several statements, including claims that the developer was:

- suitable to buy the land
- suitable to build the property
- the estate agent's Spanish agent.

None of these were terms of the contract with the developer so there was no action for breach of contract. The case was brought on the basis of misrepresentation. The next question was therefore whether the statements above were misrepresentations.

- The first statement was true.
- The second statement was not true, but the British estate agent had been to Spain to see the developer at work and did not have any reason to suspect his honesty.
- The third statement was untrue.

1. What are the rules for a statement to be a misrepresentation?

2. Was the first statement a misrepresentation?

3. Was the second statement a misrepresentation?

4. Was the third statement a misrepresentation?

5. What type(s) of misrepresentation were any of these statements?

Activity 1.9 Sample scenario problem questions

These questions reflect the style of question you are likely to see in your exams for Eduqas A Level Component 2 and WJEC A Level Unit 3.

Apply the law on misrepresentation and economic duress to these scenarios.

Misrepresentation scenario

Liam went to buy a washing machine. He wanted a model that could do express washes. He went into a branch of his local electrical store and asked for the manager, Jon, to give him advice. Jon told him that the best washing machine had a fast wash cycle of 15 minutes and could wash at a low temperature of 30°C. Liam accepted the advice and bought the machine. When the washing machine was delivered, Liam discovered that it took 45 minutes to complete the wash cycle and that the water temperature could only be set at 60°C. As a result, Liam's electricity bill doubled.

Liam wishes to reject the machine. Advise him.

Misrepresentation and economic duress scenario

Nell entered into a contract to deliver fence panels to Bailey. After two weeks of making deliveries, Nell realised that she had miscalculated how many fence panels could be carried in an average load on her lorry and, because fuel prices were increasing, she was going to lose money on the contract and go out of business. Nell told Bailey about her problems. It was very important to Bailey that he receive the regular fence panel deliveries from Nell because he needed a large quantity to fulfil a housing development contract. Reluctantly therefore, he agreed to pay Nell more for the fence panels. Having now built the houses, he has decided not to pay the increased price to Nell.

Advise Nell.

Activity 1.10 Misrepresentation and economic duress

1. Identify four statements that could be classed as misrepresentations in the sale of a car.

2. Identify four instances that could be considered economic duress in the formation of a contract in which a major sports brand will supply rugby boots to an independent sports shop.

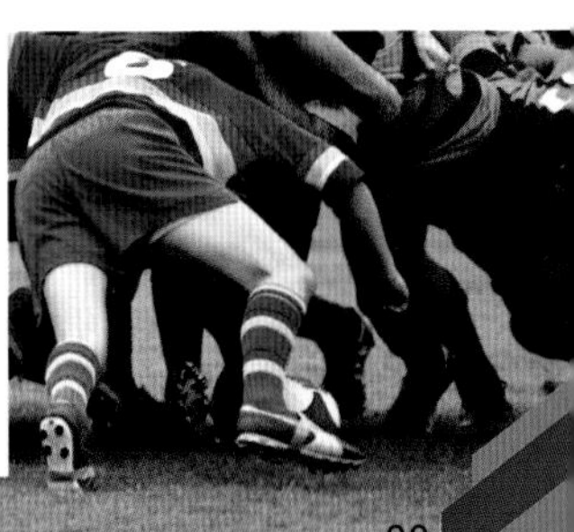

1.2 Quickfire questions

1. What is **misrepresentation** under contract law?
2. What are the essential requirements of a misrepresentation?
3. What remedies are available for negligent misrepresentation?
4. What are the **three** different types of misrepresentation?
5. According to the case of ***Pao On v Lau Yiu Long (1980)***, what must be checked before the validity of a claim of economic duress can be established by the courts?
6. What is the effect of a court finding a misrepresentation?
7. Are remedies always available for misrepresentation?
8. What happens if the statement was not made by one party of the contract to the other?
9. What is classed as a **statement of fact**?
10. What is **economic duress**?

CHAPTER 2 THE LAW OF TORT

Torts connected to land

EDUQAS A-LEVEL

Spec spotlight	In this section students will develop their knowledge of:
Eduqas A Level 2.2.4: Torts connected to land	• Trespass to land: unlawful entry, intention, defences of lawful authority, including licence, right of entry • Public nuisance: class of persons, role of Attorney General, when an individual can sue • Private nuisance: unlawful interference / physical damage, interference with health and comfort, unreasonable user, relevance of locality and utility, abnormal sensitivity; duration; effect of malice • Specific defences to nuisance: prescription; statutory authority • ***Rylands v Fletcher (1868)***: dangerous things; accumulation, escape, non-natural user, damage • Specific defences: consent, act of stranger, statutory authority, act of God, default of claimant

Revision booster

This topic could feature as a scenario-type question testing **AO2 application** skills. For this type of question, you need to advise someone in relation to the issues, for example on an application of the rules on trespass to land, public and private nuisance, the rule in ***Rylands v Fletcher*** or defences. For these longer responses, you should start your answer with an introduction that provides an overview of the topic areas, and end it with a conclusion that ties together the issues based on your application of the evidence. As **AO2** is the skill being tested, it is essential to apply the law to the scenario provided, using cases and statutes to support your argument.

This topic could also feature as an essay question testing **AO3 analysis and evaluation** skills. Think about the elements of each topic that could warrant a higher mark, more evaluative response. Some possible questions might be as follows:

- 'The tort of private nuisance is ineffective and has little relevance in the modern law of torts.' Discuss the tort of private nuisance in relation to this statement.
- 'The tort of Rylands v Fletcher is so complex for all the parties concerned that it has become ineffective.' Discuss the extent to which this statement is accurate.

For these longer responses, you should start with an introduction that provides an overview of what the answer is going to discuss and how the main body will progress. It should also provide some brief context, along with an explanation of key terms in relation to the topic or question. Your answer should then follow a logical paragraphed structure with a link back to the question and evidence used to support your answer. Finally, it should have a conclusion that ties together the issues based on the evidence you have presented and with reference to the question. In order to evaluate, you also need to explain what it is you are evaluating.

LINK

For more on torts connected to land, see pages 26–43 of *WJEC/ Eduqas A Level Law Book 2.*

Build your revision notes around...

- **Trespass to land**
  - Four essential elements:
    - direct interference with the land
    - the interference must be voluntary
    - no need for defendant to be aware they were trespassing
    - no need for claimant to experience harm or loss
  - Three main defences: legal authority (justification by law), consent, necessity
  - Remedies: damages and injunctions, orders for possession, self-help (abatement)
  - Trespass in criminal law: main offences: aggravated trespass and squatting
- **Private nuisance**
  - An interference with a person's **enjoyment and use** of their land
  - Is a **civil action**
  - Three kinds:
    - Nuisance by encroachment on a neighbour's land
    - Nuisance by direct physical injury to a neighbour's land
    - Nuisance by interference with a neighbour's quiet enjoyment of their land
  - Key elements:
    - Claimant must have an interest in the land
    - Must be unreasonable use of the land which is the source of the nuisance
    - Claimant must suffer some harm or inconvenience
  - Main defences: statutory authority and prescription
  - Main remedies: damages and injunctions
  - Key case: the rule from ***Rylands v Fletcher (1868)***
  - Defences: ***Rylands v Fletcher (1868)***
- **Public nuisance**
  - A nuisance that materially affects the **reasonable comfort and convenience** of life of a class of Her Majesty's subjects
  - Differs from private nuisance on the basis of who is affected. A public nuisance affects a **representative cross-section** of a class of society in a neighbourhood
  - Is a **crime**
  - No requirement of intention or recklessness: the fault element is one of **foreseeability** of the risk of the type of nuisance
  - Defendant is liable if they knew or ought to have known of the risk of the type or kind of nuisance that occurred: ***Wagon Mound (No 1) (1961)***
  - Three types of civil actions can be brought against those committing a public nuisance:
    - A realtor action
    - Under the ***Local Government Act 1972*** by a local authority
    - An action for tort by a private citizen who can show that they have suffered special damage beyond that experienced by other 'Her Majesty's subjects'

Context

Private nuisance: An unlawful interference for a substantial length of time with a person's right to enjoy or use their land in a reasonable way and is actionable in tort.

Public nuisance: A crime and a tort that seeks to protect the health, safety, morals and convenience of the public and to prevent the obstruction of any right held by every member of the public.

Activity 2.1 Private and public nuisance

Test your knowledge of public and private nuisance by using the words from the list to fill in the blanks.

Private nuisance		
Element of tort	**Law**	**Case**
Valid claimant and defendant	Claimant must be someone with a ______ interest in the land. Defendant is the creator of the nuisance or the occupier who continues the activities of the creator. ______ can be liable for actions of tenants if they authorise or approve the actions of the tenants.	***Hunter v ______:*** Claimants complained about dust and TV interference from building work. Some of the claimants were unable to pursue claims because they lacked any legal interest in the affected land. ***______ v O'Callaghan:*** A trespasser installed a pipe in a ditch on the defendant's land. Three years later, the pipe became blocked and the flooding damaged the claimant's land. Defendant was liable, even though he had not installed the pipe, as he knew of its existence. ***______ v Chitty:*** Local council was liable for the noise and disturbances caused by a go-kart club as the council had leased land to the club for the express purpose of developing a go-kart track.

Continued

Words to use
Canary Wharf
landlords
legal
Sedleigh-Denfield
Tetley

Private nuisance		
Element of tort	**Law**	**Case**
Interference	Two types of interference: (e.g. noise on one piece of land which affects the people living next door). interference (where the defendant has come onto the claimant's land). The interference usually needs to be , rather than one-off. damage to the land Loss of amenity: The claimant's ability to use or enjoy their land is restricted by the activities of the defendant (e.g. excessive preventing the claimant from getting a good night's sleep; unpleasant smells and fumes preventing the claimant from opening).	***Holbeck Hall Hotel v BC:*** Claimant's hotel was built on the council's land, and it collapsed when there was a landslide. The council had not taken reasonable precautions to prevent the landslide, but it was not held liable as the damage was not foreseeable.
Interference is unlawful	It is unreasonable: people have the right to use their own land as they wish. There is a limit beyond which activities become unlawful. Courts ask: • Does the nuisance interfere with ordinary existence? • Is the impact on the claimant so unreasonable that they should not be expected to put up with it? Courts consider several factors when deciding if it is unreasonable, including the fact that certain activities are lawful in some circumstances but not in others. • : Claimants using their property for an extra-sensitive reason are not entitled to sue where a reasonable use would not need protection.	***McKinnon v*** : Claimant could claim for the full damage caused to delicate orchids by gas emitted from the defendant's factory. Even flowers of ordinary sensitivity would have been affected. ***v Bridgman***: 'What would be a nuisance in [quiet, residential] Belgrave Square would not necessarily be so in [industrial] Bermondsey.' ***St Helens Smelting v*** : Copper smelting, even in an industrial area, could be classed as a nuisance when it resulted in smuts damaging the claimant's shrubs. ***v Stone:*** Cricket balls were rarely hit out of field but caused damage to property. Nuisance occurred very infrequently, so no breach of duty or nuisance. ***v Kimbolton Fireworks***: A firework display that set fire to some moored barges was held to be a private nuisance.

Continued

Private nuisance		
Element of tort	**Law**	**Case**
	• Locality of the events. • A nuisance claim is more likely to be if there is damage to property. • Courts are more likely to consider a nuisance unreasonable if it lasts for a long time or is during unsociable hours. • A single event can amount to a nuisance. • Social utility of defendants, conduct: Just because something is considered useful to society does not mean that a remedy is not available in nuisance. • If a nuisance is caused for reasons, the claim is more likely to succeed (e.g. the defendant deliberately does something just to annoy the claimant).The defendant's malice can make unlawful something that might not otherwise be a nuisance.	***Dennis v*** : Claimant lived in a large house in the country but his peace was regularly destroyed by RAF training jets flying overhead. Noise did amount to a nuisance and he was awarded damages, but no injunction as the flights were a necessary part of the country's defence preparations. ***Hollywood Silver Fox Farm v*** : Claimant farmed silver foxes. Defendant, as part of an ongoing feud, deliberately fired shotguns within the boundaries of his own land to startle the foxes and cause them to miscarry. Normally, firing a shotgun in the countryside would probably not be a nuisance, but here the malicious motive made it unlawful. ***Christie v*** : The defendant lived next to a house used for piano and singing lessons. The defendant was annoyed and whistled, shrieked and banged tin trays on the walls during lessons. Injunction imposed against him because it was clear he deliberately aimed to disrupt and upset. The original music making was not held to be a nuisance.

Continued

Words to use
Bolton
continuous
Crown River Cruises
Davey
Direct
Emmett
Indirect
malicious
MOD
noise
Physical
Scarborough
Sensitivity
Sturges
successful
Tipping
Walker
windows

Public nuisance		
Element of tort	**Law**	**Case**
Public nuisance	Rarely used today as most activities under public nuisance are now covered by legislation. Claimant must prove a class of people have suffered a common harm or injury. Public nuisance case will reach court in one of three ways: • By a case. Most common. Investigated by police and prosecuted by CPS. • The seeks an injunction on behalf of the public. • By a action brought by an individual who must show they suffered a special or particular damage, loss or injury beyond other members of their class.	***Halsey v*** : Oil refinery discharged oily smuts that damaged the paintwork of the claimant's car, which was parked in the street outside his house. Other cars may have been affected but the claimant suffered damage beyond that of others and was able to claim for repairs to his car's paintwork.
A class of people have been affected	It is not enough to show it affected one person. A public nuisance is one 'which materially affects the reasonable comfort and convenience of life of a class of subjects'. It covers a section of the public, rather than individuals, and should involve a considerable number of people.	***AG v*** : Quarry owner argued the 30 houses affected by the dust and noise covered too few people to constitute a class. The court disagreed but declined to give guidelines on what number constituted a class. ***R v*** : Defendant telephoned a bomb hoax to a steel works, which disrupted the business for about an hour. While a hoax telephone call falsely alleging that explosives had been planted could be an offence of public nuisance, few employees were on site and therefore there was not a sufficiently wide class of the public.

Continued

OPEN

Public nuisance		
Element of tort	**Law**	**Case**
Common harm or injury	Affects a right, a common protection or a benefit enjoyed by the members of the affected class.	***R v*** : Defendant sent out 538 packages to different people containing racially offensive material. Some victims were chosen at random; others were picked because of their ethnic background. House of Lords held it was not a public nuisance as the actions of the defendant did not cause a common injury to a section of the public. It is different if the defendant often blocks the highway for no good reason. ***Lyons v*** : Defendant committed a public nuisance as he regularly allowed large queues of people seeking cheap seats to build up on the pavement outside his theatre, impeding access to claimant's shop.
Highways	Many public nuisances occur as a result of of the right of passage over a highway. A temporary obstruction is unlikely to amount to a public nuisance unless it is also unreasonable. A person who trips over uneven paving stones will probably be to obtain compensation. The duty has limitations.	***Trent v*** : Claimant tripped over a hosepipe laid across the highway by the defendant, who had no mains water connection to his premises. Claimant's action failed as the use by the defendant was regarded as reasonable. ***Noble v*** : Where premises adjoin the highway and damage is caused by something falling onto the highway, the landowner may be liable for public nuisance if evidence shows they knew or ought to have known of the danger. ***Wringe v*** : Dangerous premises that collapse onto the highway are public nuisance if the collapse is caused by lack of maintenance. ***v Department of Transport***: There is no general common law duty to salt roads to prevent a built up of ice.

Words to use

able	criminal	Lee
abuse	Esso Petroleum	Madden
Attorney General	Gulliver	PYA Quarries
civil	Harrison	Rimmington
Cohen	Her Majesty's	Sandhar

Activity 2.2 Applying Rylands v Fletcher

Read the evaluation notes and use them to write a sample essay that will answer the question. Remember to structure your response with an introduction, reasoned arguments and a conclusion. Note that R v F = ***Rylands v Fletcher (1868)***, C = claimant, D = defendant and H of L = House of Lords.

Discuss the arguments that, in the tort of *Rylands v Fletcher*, judges have created so many separate requirements and so many defences that there is little chance of pursuing a successful claim.

- As it's a strict liability tort where C doesn't have to prove defendant is at fault, it should be much easier for C to successfully bring a claim. It's certainly easier than bringing a claim in negligence.
- But D is allowed to use various defences so R v F action is not really a strict liability tort at all. This makes it harder for C to make a successful claim.
- Requirement that D must use land in 'unnatural' way adds to C's problems. Simplest way for D to defeat claim is to show a natural use of land.
- R v F rule has been further restricted:
  - D is only liable if whatever is stored on their land escapes: Read v Lyons (1947), Wyvern Tyres (2012)
  - AND it causes foreseeable damage to C's land: Cambridge Water v Eastern Counties Leather (1994). In saying damage to C's land was unforeseeable in Cambridge Water, H of L 'sealed the fate of an already moribund tort', and this has meant even fewer R v F claims!
- R v F doesn't cover any situation that isn't already covered in other areas of tort, like negligence and private nuisance, so it's not really needed. In 1994, Australian High Court said R v F would be part of negligence. Cambridge Water described it as a type of private nuisance. As far back as 1978, Pearson Commission recommended R v F rule should be abolished.
- Parliament has created statute law to replace R v F in some areas, where C is expected to take action using statute, rather than R v F claim, i.e.:
  - Reservoirs Act 1975 covers escape of accumulated water
  - Nuclear Installations Acts 1965 and 1969 covers escape of radioactive substances.

- H of L reviewed law on R v F in Transco v Stockport Borough Council (2003): 'natural' use of land should now be interpreted as 'ordinary' use of land, so R v F rule will only apply if defendant 's use of land is extraordinary and unusual. This will make it harder still for claimant's claim to succeed.
- H of L had opportunity to abolish R v F rule in Transco case, but chose not to – said it's been in existence for 150 years and, if someone wants to get rid of it, it should be Parliament, not the courts.
- Claimant cannot claim damages for personal injury in R v F action (obiter comment in H of L Transco case above) – this further limits the tort's usefulness.

Activity 2.3 Sample answers for scenario question on nuisance and Rylands v Fletcher

Sam owned a takeaway shop selling curries in a quiet village. The customers, who often stood in long queues in and outside the shop, caused considerable noise, and there were strong smells from the cooking of the curries. Richard bought the house next to Sam's shop. When, after several months of this annoyance, Richard complained to Sam, Sam increased his opening hours.

In a separate dispute, lighter fluid, which Richard had bought for barbecues, leaked from cans in his shed into Sam's garden, destroying Sam's delicate and rare orchids.

Rhys regularly parked his large van in the narrow lane when making deliveries to Sam's shop, causing a severe obstruction for motorists in the village.

Consider the rights, if any, of:

1. Richard against Sam in connection with the noise and the smells
2. Sam against Richard in connection to the destruction of the plants
3. The motorists against Rhys in connection with the obstruction.

Identify the type of nuisance and whether the case of ***Rylands v Fletcher (1868)*** (R v F) is relevant. Explain what needs to be established in each scenario for a successful claim. Think about what should be taken into account and what the courts are likely to look for. Include relevant case examples and conclude stating whether you think the claimant is likely to have a successful case. Continue your answers on a separate piece of paper if necessary.

1. Richard against Sam:

Type of nuisance claim or R v F:

2. Sam against Richard

Type of nuisance claim or R v F:

Continued

3. Rhys's parking

Type of nuisance claim or R v F:

Activity 2.4 Nuisance law

Apply the law on nuisance to the scenario below.

Clive owns a pig farm. Six months ago, he obtained planning permission to build another large shed to expand his business. Clive's next-door neighbour, Taylor, is an artist who sells work from a studio at his home. He complains forcefully to Clive that his business is suffering because the noise and smell of the pigs means that visitors do not stay long enough to buy any art. In response, Clive takes delivery of even more pigs. Lorries deliver and collect day and night. Taylor claims the lorries keep him awake and the rural atmosphere is ruined. The cars and lorries also produce fumes that Taylor says have killed his prize-winning orchids.

Advise Taylor on whether he may have any nuisance claims against Clive and what his remedies might be.

2.1 Quickfire questions

1. Do the items that are kept and collected on the land need to be dangerous in ***Rylands v Fletcher***?
2. What does **escape** mean in ***Rylands v Fletcher***?
3. What are the possible defences that can be used in ***Rylands v Fletcher***?
4. What does a claimant need in order to make a claim in private nuisance?
5. What is **interference**?
6. What can make interference unreasonable?
7. What are the essential elements of trespass to land?

Vicarious liability

EDUQAS A-LEVEL

Spec Spotlight	In this section students will develop their knowledge of:
Eduqas A Level **2.2.5:** Vicarious liability	• Nature and purpose of vicarious liability • Liability for employees: tests for status of employment, scope of employment, 'frolic of his own' • Liability for independent contractors: distinguished from employees, choice of, and supervision in relation to, unusually hazardous activities

For more on vicarious liability, see pages 44–48 of *WJEC/Eduqas A Level Law Book 2*.

Revision booster

This topic features on Eduqas A Level specification and could feature on the law of tort section. It could feature as an **AO1 explain** question, an **AO2 apply** question or an **evaluate** question testing **AO3**.

Build your revision notes around...

- **Definition** of vicarious liability: liability of one person for the torts committed by another
  - Requirement of legal relationship between the two parties and a connected tort
  - Form of strict liability and joint liability
- **Two questions** to determine if vicarious liability applies:
  1. Is the tortfeasor **an employee**?
     - Employees v independent contractors:
       - Control test: ***Yewens v Noakes (1880)***
       - Organisation (or 'integration') test: ***Stevenson, Jordan & Harrison v MacDonald & Evans (1952)***
       - Multiple test: ***Ready Mixed Concrete Ltd v Minister of Pensions (1968)***
  2. Was the tort committed **in the course of their employment**?
     - Course of employment v 'frolic of his own':
       - Part of authorised duties: ***Century Insurance v Northern Ireland Road Transport (1942)***
       - Frolic: ***Storey v Ashton (1869)***
       - Doing authorised work in a forbidden manner: ***Limpus v London General Omnibus (1863)***
       - Travelling to work: ***Conway v Wimpey (1951)***, ***Hilton v Thomas Burton (Rhodes) Ltd (1961)***, ***Rose v Plenty (1975)***

- Reasons for imposing vicarious liability:
  - Employer finances
  - Employers in control of conduct of employees
  - Employers profit from work of employees
  - Employers should take care when recruiting
  - Employers encouraged to provide a safe work environment/policies

Activity 2.5 Vicarious liability

Use the words from the list to fill in the blanks to explain how vicarious liability is applied.

Words to use
another
authority
claimant
compensate
connected
course
employee
employer
employment
fault
insured
joint
justifications
negligence
relationship
responsibility
sued
unfair
strict

Vicarious liability is the term used to explain the liability of one person for the torts committed by ________. There must be a legal ________ between the two parties and the tort should be ________ to that relationship. It mostly arises in employment when an ________ might be liable for the torts of their ________. Vicarious liability is a form of ________ liability, where an employer can be liable for the actions of their employees, even though the employer is not at ________ in any way. Strict liability has the potential to be ________ but there are ________ for the imposition of such liability. For example, if someone for whom an employer has a degree of ________ over makes a mistake, then the employer bears some ________ for this.

Vicarious liability has become a practical tool to help ________ victims, as employers are often ________ against such losses. Vicarious liability is, therefore, a form of ________ liability. This means that both the person who committed the tort, and their employer, can be ________ (though in practice it is usually only the employer that is sued, because they are most likely to have insurance).

There are two questions to determine if vicarious liability applies to an employer:

1. Is the person who committed the tort an employee?

2. Was the tort committed in the ________ of that person's ________?

Of course, there primarily has to be a tort committed by the employee and, therefore, the ________ must prove the elements of whichever tort is alleged. For example, if the claimant is suing for ________, they need to establish duty, breach and resulting damage.

Activity 2.6 Elements of vicarious liability crossword

Complete the word puzzle using the clues.

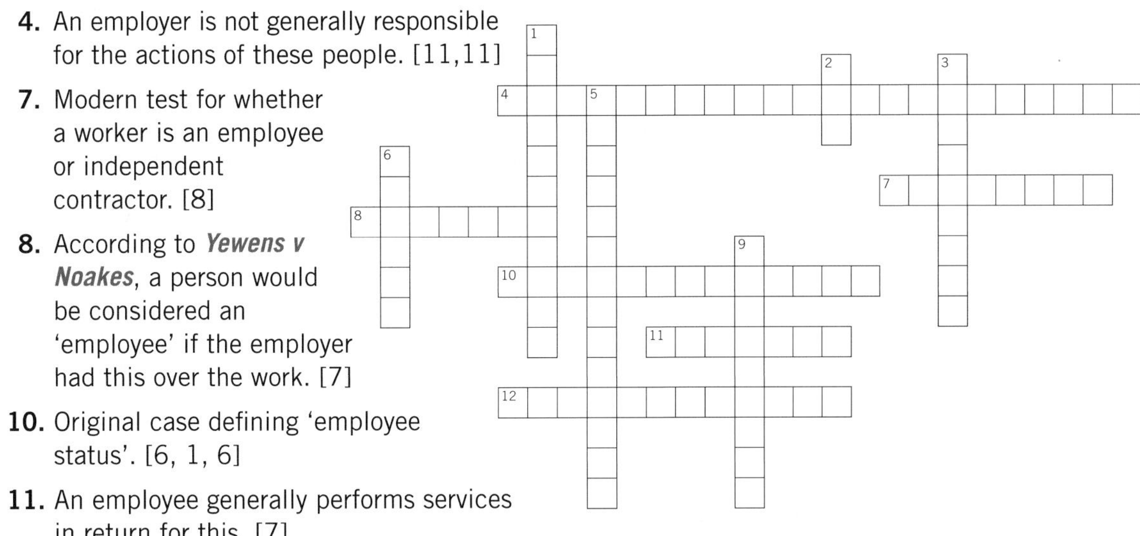

Across

4. An employer is not generally responsible for the actions of these people. [11,11]

7. Modern test for whether a worker is an employee or independent contractor. [8]

8. According to ***Yewens v Noakes***, a person would be considered an 'employee' if the employer had this over the work. [7]

10. Original case defining 'employee status'. [6, 1, 6]

11. An employee generally performs services in return for this. [7]

12. Test for 'employee status' developed in ***Stevenson, Jordan and Harrison v MacDonald and Evans (1952)***. [12]

Down

1. The name for the test used to determine who has employee status. [7,4]

2. Name of the injured person in the 2016 Supreme Court case against the Ministry of Justice that considered the nature of the relationship between an organisation and employee. [3]

3. Modern working has caused difficulties for defining who is an employee. This type of person may be regarded as self-employed but could be contracted to do a particular job independently. [9]

5. This is what the claimant must have to be considered an 'employee'. [8,5]

6. An employer is not liable for the torts committed by an employee who is on a '   of his own'. [6]

9. The term for travelling to work and back home again, which is not normally considered an activity within the course of employment. [9]

Activity 2.7 Reasons for imposing vicarious liability

It is also important to be able to evaluate the law in this area. Some of the main justifications for vicarious liability are given below. Draw lines to match the reason with its corresponding explanation.

Reason	Explanation
Insurance	Employers are in control of the conduct of employees and so should be responsible for their actions. Problems with this argument arise when considering more modern and flexible working arrangements.
Employer responsibility	Employers have control over who they employ and are in control of who is dismissed. They should be deterred from employing those known to create a 'risk'.
Profit	Employers profit from the work done by their employees so arguably should be liable for their torts and losses.
Control over risk	Employers are in a stronger financial position to pay compensation, and they will usually be insured.
Possibility of taking precautions	Employers are encouraged to take care to prevent accidents and to provide a safe working environment and good health and safety practices.

2.2 Quickfire questions

1. What is vicarious liability?
2. Why is it an important extension of the law?
3. What type of liability is it?
4. Name the **two** questions to determine if vicarious liability applies to an employer.
5. Summarise the main reasons for imposing vicarious liability.

Defences: Tort

Spec Spotlight	In this section students will develop their knowledge of:
Eduqas A Level **2.2.6:** Defences – Tort	• *Volenti non fit injuria:* must be voluntary, effect of ***Road Traffic Act 1988***, position of rescuers • Contributory negligence: nature and effect, ***Law Reform (Contributory) Negligence Act 1945***

LINK

For more on defences in the law of tort, see pages 49–51 of *WJEC/Eduqas A Level Law Book 2*.

Revision booster

This topic features on Eduqas A Level specification and could feature in the law of tort section. It could feature as an **AO1 explain** question, an **AO2 apply** question or an **evaluate** question testing **AO3**.

Build your revision notes around...

- Consent: *Volenti non fit injuria:* voluntary assumption of risk
  - ***Morris v Murray (1991)***
  - Complete defence
  - Requirements:
    - Tort
    - Knowledge of extent and nature of risk
    - Voluntary acceptance of risk
  - Passengers in vehicles: courts' reluctance to allow *volenti*
    - ***s149(3) Road Traffic Act 1988***
  - Sporting activities / spectators
    - Rules of the game: ***Smoldon v Whitworth and Nolan (1997)***
- Contributory negligence
  - Apportionment of blame and damages
  - ***Section 1(1) of the Law Reform (Contributory Negligence) Act 1945***
  - ***Sayers v Harlow UDC (1957)***
  - Employers should take care when recruiting
  - Employers encouraged to provide a safe work environment / policies

Context

Once all the elements of a tort have been proved, the defendant may escape liability by relying on a defence. The specification requires knowledge of three defences: consent *(volenti non fit injuria)*, contributory negligence and the defences specific to claims connected to nuisance and ***Rylands v Fletcher.***

Activity 2.8 Consent (*volenti non fit injuria*)

Use the words below to fill in the blanks to complete this summary of *volenti non fit injuria*.

Words to use
accepted
assumption
aware
choice
complete
consented
consents
contributory
drunk
harm
injury
knew
losses
Murray
risk
risks
Smoldon
spectators
tort
voluntarily

The Latin term *volenti non fit injuria* translates as: 'there can be no ______ to one who ______', although it is often said to mean 'voluntary ______ of risk'. The principle behind this defence is that if the claimant consented to behaviour that carries a ______ of ______ then the defendant is not liable in tort. Successfully claiming this defence means that the defendant is not liable for any of the claimant's ______. It is a ______ defence, therefore, and the claimant receives no damages.

The use of this defence can be seen in the case of ***Morris v ______ (1991)***. On appeal, the defence successfully argued that as the claimant was ______ of the risk he was taking and ______ to it, there was no liability in negligence.

In order to argue the defence, it must first be shown that the defendant has committed a ______. Once this is proved, the defendant must then prove that the claimant ______ of the risk involved (the nature and extent of the risk) and that he ______ accepted that risk (it was claimant's own free ______).

Passengers in vehicles

The courts have been reluctant to allow the *volenti* defence in cases of negligent driving, even if a passenger accepts a lift with an obviously ______ driver. ***Section 149(3) Road Traffic Act 1988*** states: 'The fact that a person so carried has willingly accepted as his the risk of negligence on the part of the user shall not be treated as negating any such liability of the user.'

There may, instead, be a defence of ______ negligence.

Sporting activities

Individuals who voluntarily participate in a sporting activity, by implication, consent to the ______ involved in that particular sport. These will vary with different sporting activities, for example, rugby tackles, cricket balls, boxing, etc. The general principle is that, provided the activity is within the rules of the game, an injured player cannot sue, as in ______ ***v Whitworth and Nolan (1997)***.

There are also some sports that carry risks for the ______, such as, being hit by a rugby ball while watching a match. The approach by the courts seems to be that an error of judgement or lapse of skill does not give rise to liability, as the spectator has ______ the risks by going to watch the live activity.

Activity 2.9 Contributory negligence

Use the words below to fill in the blanks to complete this summary of contributory negligence.

Unlike *volenti,* which is a complete defence, the defence of contributory negligence allows a court to blame (and therefore damages) between the two parties. It means that the claimant and defendant are to blame for the damage suffered, for example, if a negligent driver hits someone who had stepped into the road without looking.

Section 1(1) of the Law Reform (Contributory) Act 1945 states:

'where any person suffers damage as the result partly of his own fault and partly of the fault of any other person or persons, a claim in respect of that damage shall not be defeated by reason of the fault of the person suffering the damage, but the damages recoverable in respect thereof shall be reduced to such extent as the court thinks just and equitable having regard to the claimant's share in the responsibility for the damage.'

This means that the claimant can still make a claim against the defendant, but any damages awarded will be by the amount the claimant was to . This can be seen in the case of ***v Harlow UDC (1957)***, where the claimant's damages were reduced by 25% for her own 'blameworthiness' for standing on the toilet-roll holder.

For a defence of contributory negligence to succeed it must be proved that the claimant:

- to take care of their own safety in a way that at least caused their injuries **and**
- failed to recognise that they was risking their own safety even though 'the person' would do so.

Words to use
apportion
blame
failed
negligence
partially
partly
reasonable
reduced
Sayers

2.3 Quickfire questions

1. What is a **complete** defence?
2. What might be reduced if contributory negligence is found?
3. What is **contributory negligence**?
4. Define the term ***volenti non fit injuria***.
5. What is the position regarding *volenti* and sporting events?

CHAPTER 3 CRIMINAL LAW

Fatal offences against the person

Spec spotlight	In this section students will develop their knowledge of:
WJEC A Level **3.14:** Offences against the person **Eduqas A Level** **2.3.3:** Offences against the person (non-fatal)	• Fatal offence of murder: elements and application of law • Fatal offence of involuntary manslaughter: elements and application of law, including constructive manslaughter, gross negligence manslaughter • Fatal offence of voluntary manslaughter: elements and application of law, defences of loss of control and diminished responsibility

LINK

For more on non-fatal offences, see page 52–61 of *WJEC/Eduqas A Level Law Book 2*.

Revision booster

All assessment objectives are assessed with this topic: **AO1 knowledge**, **AO2 application** and **AO3 analysis and evaluation**. This topic could feature as an **explain**, **apply** or **evaluate** question on different areas of the specifications. You might need to explain the various fatal offences (actus reus and mens rea with case law) and/or you may have to apply these elements to a scenario where you have to decide which offence(s) have been committed.

It might be that the likely offence is murder but that there is a special defence to reduce this to voluntary manslaughter. There may also be a second offence of involuntary manslaughter from a *novus actus interveniens* that might need to be discussed. Alternatively, you may need to **analyse** and **evaluate** the law on fatal offences by considering whether the law is suitable for a scenario or in need of reform. It is likely that more than one fatal offence will feature in a scenario and you may also be required to bring in a general or special defence. Diminished responsibility and loss of control are covered in this section of this book.

Build your revision notes around...

Murder

- 'The unlawful killing of a reasonable person in being and under the King's (or Queen's) peace and with malice aforethought, express or implied' LJ Coke
- Actus reus elements:
  - Human being: independent of mother: ***AG's Reference No 3 of 1994***
  - Death: ***R v Malcherek and Steel (1981)***
  - Causation in fact: 'but for test': ***R v White (1910)***; de minimis rule: ***Pagett (1983)***
  - Legal causation:
    - injury as the operative and substantial cause of death: ***R v Smith (1959)***, ***R v Jordan (1956)***
    - 'thin-skull test': ***R v Blaue (1975)***
    - foreseeable intervening act: ***R v Roberts (1971)***

Summary: Fatal offences against the person

- Mens rea elements: malice aforethought: intention to kill OR intention to cause GBH: ***DPP v Smith (1961)***
  - Direct intention
  - Oblique intention: ***R v Woollin (1998)***: virtual certainty test

Voluntary manslaughter

- Murder elements + special defence: ***Homicide Act 1957***, ***Coroners and Justice Act 2009***
- Partial defence:
  - **Loss of control**: ***s54 Coroners and Justice Act 2009***: Loss of control, qualifying trigger, reasonable person, prosecution to disprove
  - **Diminished responsibility**: ***s52 Coroners and Justice Act 2009:*** abnormality of mental functioning, arising from a recognised medical condition must be a significant contributory factor to the killing that impaired defendant's ability to:
    - understand the nature of their conduct; or
    - form a rational judgement; or
    - exercise self-control
  - **Suicide pact**
- Defence to prove on the balance of probabilities, using expert evidence

Involuntary manslaughter

- Actus reus of murder + either unlawful and dangerous act OR gross negligence
  - **Unlawful and dangerous act**: elements of actus reus of murder
  - **Unlawful act**: act not omission; criminal act not civil
  - **Dangerous act**: reasonable person
  - Causation
  - Mens rea is the mens rea of the unlawful act

Gross negligence manslaughter

- ***R v Adomako (1994)***
  - Elements of actus reus of murder
  - Duty of care
  - Grossly negligent breach of that duty of care
  - Risk of death

Context

Murder is the most serious of all the offences of homicide. The definition of murder is not contained in statute; it is a common law offence, defined by **Lord Justice Coke** in the 17th century as:

'the unlawful killing of a reasonable person in being and under the King's (or Queen's) Peace and with malice aforethought, express or implied'.

Activity 3.1 Actus reus of murder

Use the words form the list to fill the blanks.

Words to use
Blaue
blood transfusion
brain
break
but for
causation
de minimis
died
find
independently
interveniens
Jordan
minimal
novus
operating
poisoned
police
Pagett
Smith
Steel
substantial
White

1. A human being is dead

A person is a human being when they can exist ______ of their mother. Therefore, a person who kills an unborn child may be criminally liable under the law but not of homicide. There is much controversy over what constitutes 'dead' but it seems that the courts favour the definition of ' ______ -dead' and this was confirmed in the case of ***R v Malcherek and*** ______ ***(1981).***

It must then be proved that the defendant caused the death both in fact and in law. These are known as factual and legal causation.

Factual causation is decided using the ' ______ ' test. This asks 'but for' the conduct of the defendant, would the victim have ______ as and when they did? If the answer is no then the defendant will be liable for the death. This test is demonstrated in the case of ***R v*** ______ , where the defendant ______ his mother but she died of a heart attack before the poison had a chance to take effect. He was not liable for her death.

Another part of factual causation is the ______ rule. This test requires that the original injury caused by the defendants' action must be more than a ______ cause of death. This is demonstrated in the ***R v*** ______ case, where the defendant's action was more than a minimal cause of death, even though the ______ fired shots between the defendant shooting and the victim dying.

Continued

Legal causation asks whether the injury at the time of death is still the ______ and ______ cause of death. This is demonstrated in the case of ***R v*** ______, where a soldier had been stabbed, was dropped twice while being taken to hospital, was delayed in seeing a doctor and subsequently given poor medical treatment. The court held that these other factors were not enough to ______ the chain of ______. At the time of death, the original wound was still the 'operating and substantial' cause of death. An alternative outcome where the original wound had almost healed was seen in the case of ***R v*** ______. An act that breaks the chain of causation is known as a ______ actus ______.

Another part of legal causation is the 'thin-skull' test. This means that a defendant has to take their victim as they ______ them, meaning that if the victim dies of some unusual or unexpected physical or other condition, the defendant is still responsible for the death. This is demonstrated in the case of ***R v*** ______. In this case, the defendant stabbed a woman who happened to be a Jehovah's witness. As a result of her beliefs, she refused a ______ which would have saved her life. The defendant argued he should not be responsible for her death as the procedure could have saved her life and she refused it. The court disagreed and said he must take his victim as he finds them.

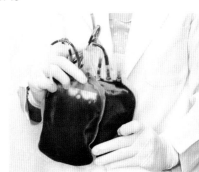

Activity 3.2 Mens rea of murder crossword

Complete the word puzzle using the clues.

Across

1. Case confirming the test for oblique intent. [6]
5. The mens rea for murder. [6,12]
7. The type of intention that is not direct. [6]
8. Example of a killing that is not malicious but satisfies the actus reus and mens rea of murder. [8,7]
9. Case where a man shot his stepfather with a shotgun as a dare. [7]
10. There is no requirement that the killing be malicious, nor this. [12]

Down

1. Penalty for murder. [4,12]
3. The current test for oblique intent. [7,9]
4. Literal translation of mens rea. [5,4]
6. Malice aforethought has come to mean an intention to kill or cause this. [1,1,1]

Activity 3.3 Reforms and criticisms of murder convictions

Use the words below to fill in the blanks to complete this summary of issues around murder convictions.

Words to use
certainty
death
degree
discretionary
euthanasia
GBH
Law Commission
mandatory x 2
manslaughter
murder
oblique
statutory
tiers

Criticisms

1. The ______ life sentence.
2. No precise definition of when ' ______ ' occurs.
3. Intention includes an intention to cause ______ but the conviction is the same (______).
4. No clear definition of intention. Problems with ______ intent.
5. Cases of ______.

Reform proposals

These have been put forward by the ______.

1. Three ______ of homicide: first-degree murder , second- ______ murder and ______.
2. Different sentences for the three tiers: ______ life imprisonment for murder and a ______ life sentence for the other two tiers.
3. Replace the common law approach to intention with a ______ definition, therefore clarifying the position regarding oblique intent and the virtual ______ test.

Context

Voluntary manslaughter is where a defendant has committed murder but is relying on a special defence contained in the ***Homicide Act 1957*** and the ***Coroners and Justice Act 2009***. If the special defence is proved, the charge of murder will be reduced to manslaughter, and the judge will have discretion in sentencing the defendant. The burden of proof is on the defence to prove that the defence applies to them.

The two special defences on the specification are:

- Loss of control
- Diminished responsibility

Activity 3.4 Voluntary manslaughter

Complete the tables to explain the key points around voluntary manslaughter in relation to loss of control and diminished responsibility. Provide at least one supporting case for each element.

Loss of control: *s54 Coroners and Justice Act 2009*

Element	Explanation	Supporting case
Loss of self-control		
Qualifying trigger		
Would another reasonable person have acted in the same way?		

Diminished responsibility: *s52 Coroners and Justice Act 2009*

Element	Explanation	Supporting case
Abnormality of mental functioning		
Arising from a recognised medical condition		
The abnormality of mental functioning must be a significant contributory factor to the killing		
The abnormality of mental functioning must have substantially impaired the defendant's ability to understand the nature of their conduct; or form a rational judgement; or exercise self-control		

Context

Involuntary manslaughter is where a defendant has committed the actus reus of murder but does not have the mens rea.

There are two forms of involuntary manslaughter in the specification:

1. Manslaughter by an unlawful and dangerous act (constructive manslaughter).
2. Gross negligence manslaughter.

Activity 3.5 Constructive manslaughter (unlawful and dangerous act manslaughter)

Fill in the missing words from the list provided.

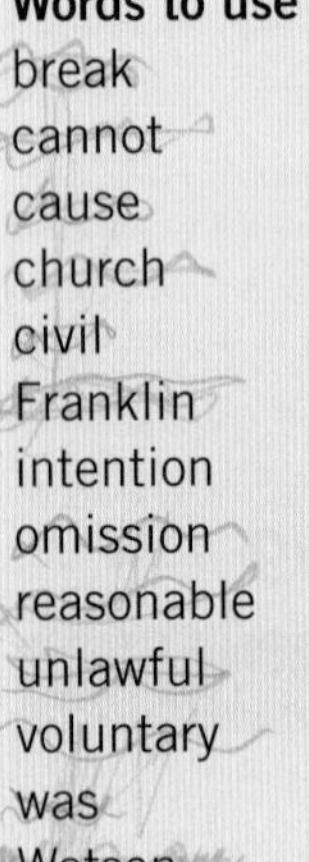

Words to use

break
cannot
cause
church
civil
Franklin
intention
omission
reasonable
unlawful
voluntary
was
Watson

The actus reus of constructive act manslaughter requires there to be an unlawful act rather than an ______ (***R v Lowe***). In addition, it must be a criminal wrong rather than ______, as decided in the case of ***R v*** ______. The act must also be dangerous by the standards of the '______ person'. This was decided in the case of ***R v*** ______.

The defendant must have the same knowledge as a sober and reasonable person. In the case of ***R v Dawson***, the victim was a 60 year old with a serious heart condition. Neither the defendants nor a sober and reasonable person could have known this. Therefore, the act ______ be dangerous. However, in the case of ***R v*** ______, the victim was an 87 year old. The court held that the defendants should be reasonably expected to know that the man would be frail and easily scared; therefore the act ______ dangerous.

Then, it must be established that the unlawful and dangerous act was the ______ of the death. If the victim intervenes into the chain of causation with a ______ act, then this will be sufficient to ______ the chain of causation – for example, in ***R v Cato***. The mens rea for this offence is the mens rea of the ______ act. For example, if the unlawful act was in ***s18 Offences Against the Person Act 1861***, then the mens rea would be ______.

Activity 3.6 Gross negligence manslaughter word search

Find the key words relating to gross negligence manslaughter in the word search.

```
E L P I C N I R P R U O B H G I E N
A S E M W G X Z V D Z R Y X W N D K
N S L R D R D K I Y I T J M N Y T K
A O T N A M T S L S Y W B Y T B M T
E R T N R C R L K T D P D W M R R R
S G X T E E F O E C N E G I L G E N
T D R B G M F O A N H Z X P G P M J
H J M A B D H D Y C J W N Y L L M N
E B R K E Y O S A T T K B M N P T K
T D L A B M B E I Y U N Q Q D G Z B
I D T M A B R R N N X D Z J Z M T T
S H G K J B B T W D U V Q N N M J Y
T T O Q D D V Z G M J P N T R R Z P
```

Words to find

ADOMAKO
ANAESTHETIST
BREACH
DISREGARD
DUTY OF CARE
GROSS
NEGLIGENCE
NEIGHBOUR PRINCIPLE
PUNISHMENT
RISK OF DEATH

Now provide a definition for the words in the word search, in relation to gross negligence manslaughter.

Negligence	
Punishment	
Gross	
Duty of care	
Neighbour principle	
Breach	
Adomako	
Anaesthetist	
Risk of death	
Disregard	

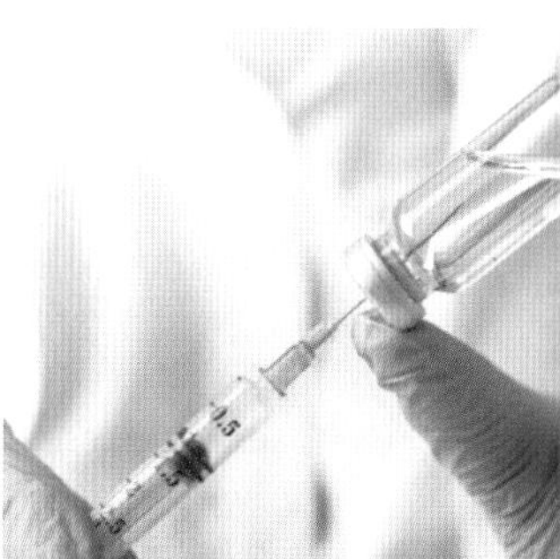

Context

When applying the law on fatal offences against the person, you are likely to be presented with a scenario that features more than one offence or the possibility of more than one offence. You need to deal with each separately, identifying the relevant offence, explaining and applying the actus reus and the mens rea in order to conclude whether the offence has been committed. Special defences are likely to feature, and you need to understand the implications of using one of these. You may also need to consider some general defences such as intoxication, which are considered in a later chapter.

Activity 3.7 Which offence? Application preparation

Fill in the tables to summarise the key points of the scenarios.

Example scenario 1

A charity which helps ex-offenders began renovating an old house in an affluent suburb of a town, to turn it into a hostel for former prisoners. Many of the people who lived nearby were opposed to the hostel, as they feared that its presence would affect the value of their own houses and make them harder to sell. One local resident, David, decided to take matters into his own hands. Under cover of darkness, he broke into the hostel and began to damage the renovation work and throw paint over the walls. Suddenly, one of the charity workers, Marla, appeared with her mobile phone in her hand, ready to call the police. To stop her, David punched her as hard as he could, knocking her unconscious. Thinking he had killed her, David tried to make it look as if Marla had died in an arson attack, by setting fire to a heap of rags before he ran from the burning building. However, Marla's phone had already connected with the emergency services before she became unconscious, and the ambulance and fire brigade arrived within minutes. Marla was brought out alive from the building, but died when the ambulance taking her to hospital was involved in a serious road accident.

Advise David as to whether he may be criminally liable for the death of Marla, applying your knowledge and understanding of legal rules and principles. (WJEC new specification SAMS)

Person / incident	Offence	Actus reus	Mens rea	Cases	Possible defence or other issues (e.g. causation)

Continued

Example scenario 2

Jason was driving along a motorway when he was suddenly forced to swerve on to the hard shoulder to avoid being hit by a van being driven by Brian. Furious, Jason chased after the van and rammed it from behind. The impact of the collision caused Brian to lose control of the van and crash into the concrete pillar of a motorway bridge, and he suffered serious injuries to his head and chest. The emergency services quickly arrived on the scene, and the air ambulance was summoned to take Brian to hospital by helicopter. Brian was placed in the helicopter under the care of Amy, a paramedic, who administered oxygen to him throughout the flight. However, as the helicopter was coming in to land, Brian's condition began to deteriorate sharply. Amy panicked and increased the amount of oxygen that Brian was receiving. This was the wrong thing to do, and Brian later died from a combination of the injuries sustained in the accident and the excessive level of oxygen in his brain.

In the light of reported case law and other sources of law, consider whether Jason might be criminally liable for the death of Brian. (WJEC LA3 June 2014)

Person / incident	Offence	Actus reus	Mens rea	Cases	Possible defence or other issues (e.g. causation)

Example scenario 3

Anna disliked her neighbour Sal because she believed Sal was responsible for killing her rabbit. They had been arguing for the last year or so. Anna decided to kill Sal, and invited her around to her house on the pretence of making up with her. When Sal arrived, Anna attacked her and hit her several times over the head with a hockey stick. Incorrectly believing Sal to be dead, she wrapped Sal in a sleeping bag and drove to a nearby village, where she threw Sal's body in a pond.

A few minutes later, PC Dollard, who was on patrol, saw Sal floating in the pond and immediately radioed for an ambulance. Sal was rushed to hospital but on the way the ambulance collided with some stray cows. Sal was thrown from the ambulance and broke her arm. When she finally arrived at the hospital, the doctor who examined her, Dr Peters, treated Sal's arm but failed to notice her fractured skull from Anna's attack. Sal died later that night.

In the light of reported case law and other sources of law, consider whether Anna may be criminally liable for Sal's death. (WJEC LA3 June 2017)

Continued

Person / incident	Offence	Actus reus	Mens rea	Cases	Possible defence or other issues (e.g. causation)

3.1 Quickfire questions

1. What is a **special defence** and what effect does it have?
2. What is the sentence for murder?
3. What is the actus reus of murder?
4. When does a person become a **human being** in law?
5. What law reformed the defence of provocation?
6. What are the elements of gross negligence manslaughter?
7. What is the mens rea for constructive manslaughter?
8. What is the current law on oblique intent for murder? Name a related case.
9. List the main problems with the law on homicide.
10. Identify three ways in which the law on homicide could be reformed and improved.

Property offences

Spec spotlight	In this section students will develop their knowledge of:
WJEC A Level **3.15:** Property offences **Eduqas A Level** **2.3.4:** Property offences	• Theft and robbery: actus reus (appropriation, property, belonging to another), mens rea (dishonesty, intentions to permanently deprive), (***s1 Theft Act 1968***) • Robbery: theft with use or threat of force (***s8 Theft Act 1968***) • Burglary: elements of ***s9(1)(a)*** and ***s9(1)(b) Theft Act 1968***, burglary in dwellings and other buildings

Revision booster

All assessment objectives are assessed with this topic: **AO1 knowledge**, **AO2 application** and **AO3 analysis and evaluation**. This topic could feature as an **explain**, **apply** or **evaluate** question on different areas of the specifications. You might need to explain the various property offences (actus reus and mens rea with case law) and/or you may then need to apply these elements to a scenario where more than one property offence might have been committed.

Alternatively, you may be required to **analyse** and **evaluate** property offences, considering whether the law is suitable or in need of reform. It is likely that more than one property offence will feature in a scenario and you may also be have to bring in a general defence (see page xxx).

LINK

For more on property offences, see pages 52–63 of *WJEC/Eduqas A Level Law Book 2*.

Build your revision notes around...

- **Theft: *s1 Theft Act 1968***
  - Maximum sentence: seven years' imprisonment
  - Triable either way offence
  - **Actus reus:**
    - ***s3***: Appropriation: bundle of rights: ***R v Morris (1923), Lawrence v MPC (1972), R v Gomez (2000), R v Hinks (2000)***
    - ***s4***: Property real property, intangible property, things in action, things that cannot be stolen: ***Oxford v Moss (1979)***
    - ***s5***: Belonging to another: possession or control, proprietary right or interest, own property (***R v Turner No.2 (1971)***), obligation to use in a particular way, mistake
  - **Mens rea:**
    - Dishonesty: ***s2*** and ***Ghosh*** test
    - Intention to permanently deprive: ***s6***: ***Lloyd (1985), Velmuyl (1989)***
- **Robbery: *s8 Theft Act 1968***
  - Maximum sentence: life imprisonment
  - Indictable offence
  - **Actus reus:**
    - Actus reus of theft: ***s1 Theft Act 1968***
    - Uses force or there is a threat of force in order to steal: ***Corcoran v Anderton (1840), Dawson and James (1976), Clouden (1987)***
    - Immediately before or at the same time as stealing: ***Hale (1979)***
    - On any person
  - **Mens rea:**
    - Mens rea of theft
    - Intention to use force in order to thieve
- **Burglary: *s9(1)(a)* and *s9(1)(b)Theft Act 1968***
  - Maximum sentence: 14 years' imprisonment
  - Triable either way offence
  - **Burglary under *s9(1)(a)*:** guilty if person enters a building, or any part of a building, as a trespasser, with intent toc ommit theft, inflict GBH on any person in the building or commit criminal damage
  - **Actus reus:**
    - Entry: ***R v Collins (1973), R v Brown (1985), Ryan (1996)***
    - Into a building (***B and S v Leathley (1979)***) or part of a building (***Walkington (1979)***)
    - As a trespasser (***Walkington (1979)***), permission to enter (***Collins (1972), Smith and Jones (1976)***)
  - **Mens rea:**
    - Intention or recklessness as to trespass
    - Ulterior intent: intention to commit theft, grievous bodily harm or damage to the building or its contents

- **Burglary under *s9(1)(b)*:** guilty if person, having entered a building or part of a building as a trespasser, steals, attempts to steal anything in the building or inflict or attempts to inflict GBH on any person in it.
- **Actus reus:**
  - Entry: ***R v Collins (1973)***, ***R v Brown (1985)***, ***Ryan (1996)***
  - Into a building (***B and S v Leathley (1979)***) or part of a building (***Walkington (1979)***)
  - As a trespasser (***Walkington (1979)***), permission to enter (***Collins (1972)***, ***Smith and Jones (1976)***)
  - Actus reus of theft or grievous bodily harm, or attempt theft or grievous bodily harm inside
- **Mens rea:**
  - Intention or recklessness as to trespass
  - Mens rea for theft or grievous bodily harm or attempt theft / grievous bodily harm inside

Context

Theft

At A Level, the topic of **property offences** covers three separate offences:

- theft
- robbery
- burglary.

Prior to the ***Theft Act 1968***, this area was covered by common law and was complex. The ***Theft Act 1968*** effectively codified the law of some property offences. It has, however, continued to evolve through the interpretation of various parts of the Act by judges deciding relevant cases. Since the original 1968 Act, there has been two further statutory updates – the ***Theft Act 1978*** and the ***Theft (Amendment) Act 1996***, which amends the 1968 and 1978 Acts.

Theft is defined in ***s1 Theft Act 1968***:

'A person is guilty of theft if he dishonestly appropriates property belonging to another with the intention of permanently depriving the other of it...'

The actus reus of theft is:

- Appropriation (***s3***)
- Property (***s4***)
- Belonging to another (***s5***)

The **mens rea of theft** is:

- Dishonesty (***s2***) and **Ghosh** test and ***Ivey v Genting Casinos***
- Intention to permanently deprive (***s6***)

The maximum sentence for theft is seven years' imprisonment.

Activity 3.8 Actus reus of theft – 'appropriation'

Fill in the missing words to help explain appropriation.

Words to use
1968
appropriation
assumption
bundle
Gomez
innocently
keep
keeping
Lawrence
lower
Morris
owner
touching
vulnerable

This element is defined in ***s3(1) Theft Act*** ____:

'Any ____ by a person of the rights of an ____ amounts to an appropriation, and this includes where he has come by the property (____ or not) without stealing it, any later assumption of a right to it by ____ or dealing with it as owner.'

This means that the defendant has physically taken an object (for example, a handbag or tablet computer) from its owner. The defendant is **assuming some or all of their rights.** This aspect has been interpreted widely and includes assuming any rights of the owner, such as moving, ____ destroying or selling. In other words, they are doing something with the property that the owner has a right to do ('____ of rights') and that no one else has the right to do without the permission of the owner. One right is sufficient, as in ***R v ____ (1923)***, where the defendant switched the price on an item, intending to pay the ____ price. Even though he did not make it to the checkout, the price switch and the placement of the goods in his trolley was considered to be an '____', as the owner has the right to price their own goods.

Section 3(1) also covers situations where someone does not steal property (for example, they are lent a bracelet by a friend) but then assumes the rights of the owner by refusing to return it. The 'appropriation' takes place once the person decides to ____ it.

An appropriation can still take place even if the victim consents to the property being taken, as in the case of ***____ v MPC (1972).*** This principle was followed in ***R v ____ (2000).***

In the case of ***R v Hinks (2000)***, the defendant's charge of theft was upheld regardless of it being a gift, as the defendant had 'appropriated' the money. This rule has the advantage of protecting ____ people.

Activity 3.9 Actus reus of theft – 'property'

Use the words from the list provided to complete the explanation of 'property' in relation to theft.

This element is defined in ***s4 Theft Act 1968***:

'Property includes money and all other property, real or personal, including things *in* action *and other* intangible *property.'*

'Property' may seem easy to define at first but there are some issues that need to be considered in further detail.

Words to use
action
chose
Electricity
information
intangible
intellectual
money
Oxford
physical
property
real
severed
things
wasted

Things that can be stolen

The following amount to property:

- Money (its physical existence rather than its value).
- Personal property.
- real property.
- Things in action.

Real property includes land and buildings, although ***s4(2)*** provides that land and things forming part of the land and severed from it (e.g. flowers, picked crops) cannot normally be stolen, except in the circumstances laid down in ***s4(2)***.

Intangible property means property that does not exist in a physical sense, such as copyright and patents.

A **'thing in action'** (also known as a 'chose **in action'**) is a technical term for property that does not exist in a physical sense but which provides the owner with legally enforceable rights. Examples include a bank account in credit (where the bank refuses the customer their money), investments, shares and intellectual property such as patents. People have legal rights over these 'things' but they cannot physically hold them.

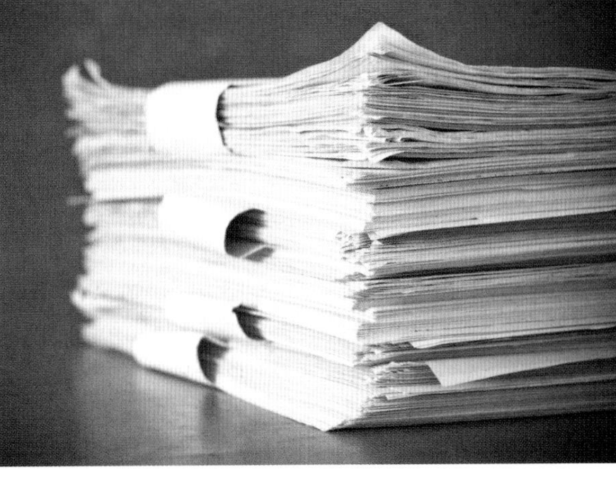

The courts have, however, decided that some things are not 'property' within the definition. In Oxford ***v Moss (1979)***, it was held that seeing unopened exam questions was not theft as they were not 'property' but 'information'.

Electricity is treated separately under the Act. It is considered intangible property that cannot be stolen but, if a person (***s11***) 'dishonestly uses electricity without authority or dishonesty causes it to be wasted or diverted' then they may be liable for an offence.

Continued

Things that cannot be stolen

Words to use
value
wild

Things that cannot be stolen are set out in sections ***4(3)*** and ***4(4)*** of the Act and cover people picking mushrooms, flowers fruit or foliage growing wild on land. This is not to be treated as theft unless it is done so for reward, sale or other commercial purpose ***(s4(3))***. ***Section 4(4)*** relates wild animals, tamed or untamed.

A human body cannot normally be stolen. ***R v Kelly and Lindsay (1998)*** held that, although a dead body is not normally property, the body parts in this case could be regarded as property because their 'essential character and value has changed'.

Activity 3.10 Actus reus of theft – 'belonging to another'

Use the words from the list provided to complete the explanation of 'belonging to another' in relation to theft.

Words to use
civil law
deliberate
liable
mistake
original
owns
particular
possession
proprietary
Reference
renter
repaired
Theft
Turner

This element is defined in ***s5*** Theft ***Act 1968***:

'Property shall be regarded as belonging to any person having possession *or control of it, or having in it any proprietary right or interest.'*

It includes where a person owns the property but also where they have **possession or control** over it or where they have a proprietary **right or interest over it**. It includes property belonging to someone under civil law and covers mere possession without rights of ownership. For example, a rented wedding suit is not owned by the person renting it but they are in control of it at the time they are in possession of it. If someone takes the rented suit from the renter, they can be said to have appropriated property belonging to the renter, even though the renter does not actually own the suit.

A person can, therefore, be **liable for stealing their own property.** In ***R v*** Turner ***No.2 (1971)***, Turner had taken his car to a garage to be repaired. After the repairs had been completed, he drove the car away without paying from where it had been parked outside the garage. The garage, being 'in possession' of his car at the time he took it meant that he was consequently liable for stealing his own car.

Even if property is legally obtained, there is still an **obligation to use it in a** particular **way** under ***s5(3)***. For example, if you gave your lecturer a payment to buy a book but they spent that money on a class trip, they have not 'used the money in the right way', so it is theft.

What about situations where property is passed to the defendant by mistake, for example, the overpayment of wages? ***Section 5(4)*** provides that property which is passed to the defendant by mistake is to be treated as 'belonging to' the original owner and, therefore, once the defendant realises the mistake and refuses to return the property, a theft takes place. The failure to return the property on realising the mistake must be deliberate (see ***Attorney General's*** Reference ***(No 1 of 1983) (1985)***).

Activity 3.11 Mens rea of theft

Complete the word puzzle using the clues.

Across

5. Intention is always this. [9]
6. The name of the case where it was stated that borrowing could fall within s6 if the property was borrowed 'until the goodness, the virtue, the practical value... has gone out of the article.' [5]
7. The intention to deprive someone of their property under s6 Theft Act must be this. [9]
8. If s2 does not apply, the case law from this applies. [5]
9. The term used for taking a car for a drive without the owner's consent without keeping it permanently. [9]

Down

1. Case where the defendant was convicted after taking cash from his employer's safe, even though he intended to replace it the next day. [7]
2. A shortened term for ' taking without consent'. [1,1,1,1]
3. As well as 'intention to permanently deprive', this needs to be proved for the mens rea of theft. [10]
4. Name of the casino in a recent case updating the Ghosh test. [7]

Context

Robbery

This offence is similar to theft but involves the use of **force** to facilitate the theft.

Robbery is defined in ***s8(1) Theft Act 1968***.

'A person is guilty of robbery if he steals, and immediately before or at the time of doing so, and in order to do so, he uses force on any person or puts or seeks to put any person in fear of being then and there subjected to force.'

It is an indictable offence meaning it is triable on indictment in the Crown Court. It is a more serious offence than theft. It can carry a maximum sentence on conviction of life imprisonment.

Activity 3.12 Robbery actus reus and mens rea

Use the prompts in the table to explain the different aspects of robbery.

Actus reus	Explanation with supporting legal authority
Appropriation	This element is defined in ***s3(1) Theft Act 1968*** ... This means that the defendant ... This aspect has been interpreted widely and includes ... One right is sufficient – ***R v Morris (1923)***. In this case ... Section 3(1) also covers situations where ... An appropriation can still take place even if ... as in the case of ***Lawrence v MPC (1972)***. Viscount Dithorne said: ... Keith LJ said: ... In the case of **R v Hinks (2000)** ...
Property	This element is defined in ***s4 Theft Act 1968*** ... Property may seem easy to define at first but there are some issues that need to be considered in further detail. Things that can be stolen ... Real property includes land and building, although ***s4(2)*** provides that ... Intangible property means ... A 'thing in action' (otherwise known as a 'chose in action') ... For example ... The courts have, however, decided that some things are not 'property' within the definition. In the case of ***Oxford v Moss (1979)*** ... Electricity is treated separately under the Act. It is considered ... There are some things that cannot be stolen. They are set out in sections ***4(3)*** and ***4(4)*** of the Act and cover situations where ... A human body cannot normally be stolen. The case of ***R v Kelly and Lindsay (1998)*** held that ...
Belonging to another	This element is defined in ***s5 Theft Act 1968*** ... It includes where a person owns the property but also ... For example, a rented wedding suit ... A person can, therefore, be liable for stealing their own property (***R v Turner No.2 (1971)***). In this case ... Even if property is legally obtained, there is still an obligation to use it in a particular way. ***Section 5(3)*** states ... For example ... In ***Hall (1972)*** ... ***Section 5(4)*** provides that property that is passed to the defendant by mistake is ...

Continued

Actus reus	Explanation with supporting legal authority
Force or threat of force	This element distinguishes robbery from theft. Examples of 'force' include ... A threat of force is also sufficient, for example... Once the theft is complete, there is a robbery. This was confirmed in the case of ***Corcoran v Anderton (1840).*** In this case ...
In order to steal	Whether there is sufficient force (or threat of force) in order to steal is a question for the jury to decide. It can include a small amount of force as confirmed in the cases of ... Force can be indirectly applied to the victim, for example ... However, it may not be considered to be 'force' as required by robbery if ... It is not a requirement that the force be ... It is important to remember that the force (or threat of such) must be used in order to steal, for example, if a defendant pushes a woman to the ground intending to rape her and ...
Immediately before or at the time of stealing	The question of how 'immediate' is immediate has been debated in courts. The courts confirmed in ... In this case, two defendants ... The Court of Appeal held that ... This rationale was followed in the case of ...
On any person	The theft does not have to happen from the person actually being threatened. For example ...
Mens reus	Explanation
Intention to permanently deprive	The defendant must intend to ... This is covered in ***s6 Theft Act 1968 ...*** Borrowing without permission ... ***Section 6(1)*** covers situations where ... But, in the case of ***Lloyd (1985)***, the court held that ... However, in the case of ***Velmuyl (1989),*** the defendant was convicted after he ...
Dishonesty	***Section 2*** does not define dishonesty but gives examples of ... All the tests above are subjective, meaning ... If none of the above apply, the test for dishonesty outlined in the ***Ghosh*** case, below, should be used ... However, it has recently been amended following ***Ivey v Genting Casinos*** ...
Intention to use force in order to thieve	Must show the defendant had intention to use force in order to thieve.

Context

Burglary

The offence of burglary is generally considered to be someone breaking into a private residence and stealing property from it. ***Section 9 Theft Act 1968*** makes it clear that it goes further than this, defining the offence as follows:

'(1) A person is guilty of burglary if—

(a) he enters any building or part of a building as a trespasser and with intent to commit any such offence as is mentioned in subsection (2) below; or

(b) having entered any building or part of a building as a trespasser he steals or attempts to steal anything in the building or that part of it or inflicts or attempts to inflict on any person therein any grievous bodily harm.

(2) The offences referred to in subsection (1)(a) above are offences of stealing anything in the building or part of a building in question, of inflicting on any person therein any grievous bodily harm, and of doing unlawful damage to the building or anything therein.'

There are in fact **two** offences of burglary under ***s9(1)(a)*** and ***s9(1)(b)***. There is also an offence under ***s10 Theft Act 1968*** of **aggravated burglary**.

The maximum sentence on conviction for burglary is 14 years if the burglar has entered a dwelling or 10 years if the burglar has entered any other building. Aggravated burglary carries a maximum of life imprisonment.

Activity 3.13 Burglary

Fill in the missing words to complete the text about the two offences of burglary.

Burglary under *s9(1)(a)*

A person is guilty of burglary under ***s9(1)(a)*** if they enter a building or any part of a building, as a trespasser, with intent to commit theft, inflict GBH on any person in the building or commit criminal damage.

The actus reus has three elements:

- entry
- building or part of a building
- as a trespasser.

The two elements of mens rea are:

- intention or recklessness as to trespass
- ulterior intent (the intention to commit theft, GBH or damage to the building or its contents).

Continued

Burglary under *s9(1)(b)*

A person is guilty of burglary under ***s9(1)(b)*** if, having entered a building or part of a building as a trespasser, they steal , attempt to steal anything in the building or inflict or attempt to inflict GBH on any person therein.

The actus reus has four elements:

- entry
- into a building or part of a building
- as a trespasser
- actus reus of theft or Grevious bodily harm, or attempt theft/grievous bodily harm therein

The Mens rea has two elements:

- intention or recklessness as to trespass
- mens rea for theft or grievous bodily harm or attempted theft / grievous bodily harm therein.

The main difference of the two offences of burglary is that, under ***s9(1)(a)***, the intention must be formed by the defendant at the time of entry, whereas under ***s9(1)(b)***, the intent to commit the ulterior offence can come later; what the defendant intends on entry is not relevant. Also ***s9(1)(a)*** covers unlawful damage , whereas ***s9(1)(b)*** does not.

Words to use

attempted
attempt
building
criminal
entry
GBH
grievous
intent
later
mens rea
partrecklessness
steal
time
trespasser
ulterior
unlawful damage

Activity 3.14 Actus reus of burglary word search

Find the key words relating to burglary in the word search.

Words to find

- ATTEMPTED
- BUILDING
- COMPLETED
- THEFT
- EFFECTIVE
- ENTRY
- EXCEEDS
- INHABITED
- PERMISSION
- R V COLLINS
- SUBSTANTIAL
- TENT
- TRESPASSER
- ULTERIOR
- VESSEL
- WALKINGTON

```
T F E H T D E T E L P M O C
N S G B E Y S Z E J S Z G D
E T N N D D R V N U Z W V Y
T D T I E E I O B X A Z N Z
N R Y E L T T S I L K T T A
Y O C L X L T I K R R V T P
T X I E R A O I B E E T P B
E Y F S N X N C S A E T U T
N F R T S G Y P V M H I L L
E W I Y T I A Z P R L N E U
L A D O V S M T R D L S I Q
L Y N M S N E R I Z S N D T
T P T E L D K N E E P J G D
T T R Y R Y G R V P Y M V S
```

Now provide a definition of the words and explanation of the cases you found in the word search, in the context of the law on theft.

Word	Definition
Entry	
Building	
Trespasser	
Effective	
Substantial	
Completed theft	
R v Collins	
Inhabited	
Vessel	
Permission	
Exceeds	
Walkington	
Ulterior	
Attempted	

Context

When applying the law on property offences, you are likely to be presented with a scenario that features more than one offence. You need to deal with each separately, identifying the relevant offence, explaining and applying the actus reus and the mens rea in order to conclude whether the offence has been committed.

Activity 3.15 Which offence? Application preparation

Use the guidance provided for Scenario 1 to help you complete the table for Scenario 2. Ensure you apply each element and example to the facts.

Example scenario 1

Eleanor and Kelsey are flat-sharing at university. They each have separate, self-contained rooms which have locks on the door. One day, when Kelsey is out working, Eleanor goes into Kelsey's room, which has been left unlocked. Eleanor wants to borrow some money for a bus ticket, so she takes some coins Kelsey has left on her desk, intending to return them before Kelsey returns home. However, Kelsey returns early, before Eleanor has a chance to replace the money.

The next day, in the shared living space, Eleanor takes Kelsey's sandwich and eats it. She then goes into the university, where she is due to sit her final exam later that day. When she gets there, she goes to see her tutor in the classroom. The tutor is not there but Eleanor spots the exam paper on the desk. She quickly takes a photo of the paper and replaces the paper where it was found.

On her way home after the exam, Eleanor is talking on her mobile phone when Oliver punches her in the face and grabs the phone from her hand.

Person/situtation	Offence	Actus reus	Mens rea
Eleanor going into Kelsey's room and taking money	Burglary ***s9(1)(a)***	• Entry • Building or part of a building • As a trespasser	• Intention or recklessness as to trespass • Ulterior intent, i.e. Intention to commit theft, grievous bodily harm or damage to the building or its contents

Continued

Person/situtation	Offence	Actus reus	Mens rea
Eleanor takes Kelsey's sandwich from their shared living area	Theft	Appropriation ***s3***: bundle of rights: ***R v Morris (1923)***, ***Lawrence v MPC (1972)***, ***R v Gomez (2000)***, ***R v Hinks (2000)*** Property ***s4***: real property, intangible property, things in action, ***Oxford v Moss (1979)***, things that cannot be stolen Belonging to another ***s5:*** possession or control, proprietary right or interest, own property: ***R v Turner No.2 (1971)***, obligation to use in a particular way, mistake	• Dishonesty: ***s2***, Ghosh test • Intention to permanently deprive: ***s6***, ***Lloyd (1985)***, ***Velmuyl (1989)***
Eleanor taking a picture of the exam paper	Theft	Appropriation ***s3***: bundle of rights: ***R v Morris (1923)***, ***Lawrence v MPC (1972)***, ***R v Gomez (2000)***, ***R v Hinks (2000)*** Property s4 – real property, intangible property, things in action, ***Oxford v Moss (1979)***, things that cannot be stolen Belonging to another ***s5:*** possession or control, proprietary right or interest, own property: ***R v Turner No.2 (1971)***, obligation to use in a particular way, mistake Cannot steal information: (***Oxford v Moss***)	• Dishonesty: ***s2***, Ghosh test • Intention to permanently deprive: ***s6, Lloyd (1985)***, ***Velmuyl (1989)***
Oliver punching Eleanor and taking her mobile phone	Robbery	Actus reus of theft: ***s1 Theft Act 1968*** Uses force or there is a threat of force in order to steal: ***Corcoran v Anderton (1840)***, ***Dawson and James (1976)***, ***Clouden (1987)*** Immediately before or at the same time as stealing: ***Hale (1979)*** On any person	• Mens rea of theft • Intention to use force in order to thieve

Example scenario 2

Evan went into a shop and picked up a cycling magazine from the shelf. He slipped it into his bag as he did not intend to pay for it. Then he spotted the shopkeeper's mobile phone behind the counter. He asked the shopkeeper, Josh, to go to look for an item for him and, while Josh was away from the counter, Evan slipped behind the partitioned area and took his mobile phone.

Later that evening, Evan, who was short of money for food, broke into his neighbour Anne's house by sticking his arm and shoulder through an open window, and took her purse.

Continued

On his way back from Anne's house, he sees Milad walking down the street and decides to beat him up as he 'didn't like the look of him'. During the beating, Milad dropped his mobile phone and Evan took the opportunity to take it.

Person/event	Offence	Actus reus	Mens rea

3.2 Quickfire questions

1. What are the actus reus elements of theft?
2. What are the mens rea elements of theft?
3. How has the case of ***Ivey v Genting Casinos*** changed the test for dishonesty?
4. How does robbery differ from theft?
5. How do the offences of burglary under ***s9(1)(a)*** and ***s9(1)(b)*** differ?
6. Is electricity capable of being stolen? Explain your answer.
7. List some of the main issues with the law on theft, robbery and burglary.
8. Identify some of the ways in which the law could be reformed and improved.

Capacity and necessity defences

Spec spotlight

WJEC A Level
3.16: Defences

3.17: Preliminary offences of attempt

Eduqas A Level
2.3.5: Capacity defences of insanity and intoxication

2.3.6: Necessity defences of self-defence, duress and duress of circumstances

In this section students will develop their knowledge of:

- Capacity defences of insanity and intoxication
- Intoxication by alcohol; Intoxication by drugs
- Insanity
- Automatism: insane and non-insane automatism
- Necessity defences of self-defence, duress and duress of circumstances
- Mistake
- Duress by threat
- Consent

LINK

For more on capacity defences, see pp74–94 of *WJEC/Eduqas A Level Law Book 2*.

Revision booster

This topic could feature as a scenario-type question testing **AO2 application** skills, where you need to advise someone in relation to the issues. A scenario question could consider an application of the rules on intoxication, insanity, automatism, self-defence, duress, mistake, necessity or consent, or a combination of several defences. For these longer responses, you should start your answer with an introduction that provides an overview of the topic areas, and end it with a conclusion that ties together the issues based on your application. As **AO2** is the skill being tested, it is essential to apply the law to the scenario provided, using cases and statutes to support your answer.

This topic could also feature as an essay question testing **AO3 analysis and evaluation** skills. Think about the elements of each topic that could gain a higher mark, more evaluative response. Some possible questions might be as follows:

- 'The law on insanity is out of date and urgently in need of reform.' Discuss.
- 'The defence of intoxication is not fit for purpose and needs to be reformed urgently.' Discuss the extent to which this statement is accurate.

For these longer responses, you should structure your answer, beginning with an introduction that provides an overview of what the answer is going to discuss and how the main body will progress. It should also provide some brief context, along with an explanation of key terms in relation to the topic or question. Your answer should then follow a logical, paragraphed structure with a link back to the question and evidence used to support it. Finally, it should have a conclusion that ties together the issues based on the evidence presented and in relation to the question posed. In order to evaluate, you also need to explain what it is you are evaluating.

Build your revision notes around...

- **Insanity and automatism**
  - Definition: ***M'Naghten (1843)***: defect of reason; disease of the mind; not know the nature and quality of the act or not know what he is doing is wrong
  - Overlap between insanity and automatism:
    - **Insanity**: defence to prove on the balance of probabilities, must have a defect of reason due to disease of the mind; if not guilty by reason of insanity, judge can make one of four orders
    - **Automatism**: defendant to raise the defence: prosecution must disprove it; must be caused by an external factor; if not guilty, the defendant is free to go
- **Intoxication**
  - **Specific intent crimes/voluntary intoxication**:
    - Guilty if the defendant has mens rea: ***Gallagher (1963)***
    - Not guilty if no mens rea.
  - **Specific intent crimes/involuntary intoxication**:
    - Guilty if the defendant has mens rea: ***Kingston (1994)***
    - Not guilty if defendant has no mens rea: ***Hardie (1984)***
  - **Specific intent crime/drunken mistake**:
    - if mistake negates mens rea, defendant is not guilty
    - If the mistake covers the need to defend oneself, it is not a defence and the defendant will be guilty for both specific and basic intent offences: ***O'Grady (1987)***, ***Hatton (2005)***
  - **Basic intent crimes/voluntary intoxication**:
    - Becoming intoxicated is a reckless course of conduct so the defendant is guilty: ***Majewski (1977)***
  - **Basic intent crimes/involuntary intoxication**:
    - Defendant has not been reckless in becoming intoxicated so is not guilty: ***Hardie (1984)***
  - **Basic intent crimes and drunken mistake:**
  - Reckless course of conduct so defendant is guilty
- **Duress**
  - Can be by threats or circumstances
  - Available for all offences except murder (***Howe (1987)***) or attempted murder (***Gotts (1992)***)
  - Must be seriousness to the threat, and death or serious injury, but can consider cumulative effect of other threats with threat of injury
  - Two tests: objective and subjective
  - Threat does not need to be immediate but it must be imminent
  - Duress is not available where the defendant knowingly joins a violent criminal gang and/or where the defendant foresaw, or should have foreseen, the risk of compulsion

- **Consent**
  - Can never be a defence to murder or ***s18 Offences Against the Person Act 1861***
  - Generally not a defence to the offences found in ***s20*** and ***s47 of the Offences Against the Person Act 1861***, but exceptions, e.g. properly conducted sports, surgery, tattoos
  - Allowed for offence of battery, and can be implied to the everyday 'jostlings' of life

- **Necessity**
  - Definition: circumstances force a person to act in order to prevent a worse evil
  - Doubts whether necessity is a defence in its own right
  - Basis of other defences, e.g. self-defence: amount of force used to defend oneself or another must be reasonable; if force was excessive, the defence will fail
  - **Criminal law:** defence of necessity only recognised as duress of circumstances: ***Dudley v Stephens (1884)***
  - **Civil cases:** recognise the defence of necessity: ***Re A (Conjoined twins) (2000)***

Activity 3.16 Applying defences to problem scenarios

The text below gives an outline example of how to respond to a scenario question about capacity and necessity defences. Use the words from the list to fill in the blanks and then use the information to write a sample response to a scenario question from a past paper, or an example of a suitable case you've found online. You may need to add or omit some of the notes, to suit the details of your scenario.

Insanity

- A defendant (D) may be able to claim the defence of insanity. The criteria is set by case law: the rules state that, at the time of committing the act, 'the party accused was labouring under such a of reason, from a of the mind, as not to know the nature and quality of the act he was doing; or, if he did know it, that he did not know he was doing what was wrong'.
- The first element is , meaning the defendant's powers of reasoning must be impaired, based on an inability to use them, not just a failure to do so. Temporary or absent mindedness does not amount to a defect of reason, as in the case of .
- In this scenario, D clearly shows that their ability to reason was impaired because [**give evidence from scenario**].
- The second element, 'disease of the mind', is a definition, not a medical one. The law is concerned whether D can be held liable for their act, not their medical condition.

Continued

- A disease of mind must be physical, not brought on by factors, e.g. drugs.
- In this scenario, D's [**give evidence from scenario**] can be seen as a 'disease of the mind', as in / ***Sullivan/Hennessey***.
- The final element is that it must be proven that D either did not know the nature/quality of their conduct, or that they knew what they were doing but not that it was legally wrong. Here, D [**give evidence from scenario]**, so it can be seen that D knew the nature/quality of their act, as illustrated by the case of where the D said 'I suppose they'll hang me for this.'
- For insanity, the burden of proof rests with the to prove that D was suffering from insanity at the time of the offence, on the balance of . It is therefore likely / not likely that D will be able to prove insanity and be deemed 'not guilty by reason of insanity', and given a special verdict. [**Give evidence from scenario**.]

Words to use
Bratty
Burgess
Clarke
confusion
defect
defect of reason
defence
Dica
disease
external x 2
Kemp
legal
M'Naghten
probabilities
Tabassum
two
valid
Windle

Automatism

- D may be able to claim the defence of automatism. This was defined in as 'an act done by the muscles without any control of the mind'.
- There are elements of this defence. The first is that D must have experienced a total loss of voluntary control and that this was caused by an factor.
- Here, D [**give evidence from scenario**], which shows they lost voluntary control. This must be a total loss, as shown in ***AG Ref No2 1992***, where the D was unable to use automatism, as the fact he was driving meant he had not lost all control.
- In the scenario, D's actions could be said to be self-induced, as D knew their conduct was likely to lead to an automatic state. As in ***Bailey***, where D had been reckless, here also D has [**give evidence from scenario**].
- D's automatic state was / was not caused by external factors due to [**give evidence from scenario]** and they would therefore be able/unable to plead the defence of automatism.

Consent

- D may attempt to use the defence of consent. To succeed, the consent must be both and informed. For consent to be valid, the victim must be deemed to have the capacity to consent. Children and those with a mental illness are deemed unable to give valid consent.
- Also, the victim must know the nature and quality of the act they are consenting to they must be aware of what exactly they are consenting to. This was shown in the case, where consenting to sex did not include consenting to contracting a sexually transmitted disease. Additionally, consent cannot be gained through fraudulent means, displayed in the case of .

Continued

- As a general rule, people cannot consent to any hurt which would include offences under ***s47***, ***s20*** and ***s18***, unless the injury/activity fits within a recognised exception such as sport, surgery, rough horseplay etc, as in the case of , where branding was seen to be the same as tattooing.
- D could attempt to use the exception of 'rough horseplay' as [**give evidence from scenario**]. This is like in the case of , in which the victim sustained a broken arm and ruptured spleen after his classmates threw him in the air. Despite the serious injuries, consent was allowed as the boys had treated the incident as a joke and there was no intention to cause injury. In the scenario, [**give evidence from scenario**].
- D could attempt to rely on the element of consent in relation to sports, due to [**give evidence from scenario**]. Consent applies to normal sports activities which are properly conducted and supervised within the rules and regulations of that sport. Here, [**give evidence from scenario**], so D did / did not go beyond this, as in the case of .
- Therefore, D would / would not be able to plead the defence of consent.

Self-defence and crime prevention

- D may be able to use the defence of self-defence. There are two types – self-defence and – under ***s3 Criminal Law Act 1967***. For the defence to apply, D must satisfy two elements; firstly, whether the force was and, secondly, whether it was . The prosecution must prove beyond reasonable doubt that either D wasn't acting in self-defence or that the force was excessive.
- Jury decides whether the force was necessary based on the facts. However, as in the case of , where the attacker was running away, force is unlikely to be necessary. In the scenario, [**give evidence from scenario**], so it can be said the force was/wasn't necessary.
- Where D has made a mistake, jury decides whether force was necessary in the circumstances that D honestly believed existed, as shown in ***Williams***. In this scenario, [**give evidence from scenario**], so it can be said the force was/ wasn't necessary in the circumstances.
- D can rely on the defence even if they have made a pre-emptive strike, as shown in ***AG No2 1993***. [**Give evidence from scenario.**]
- Whether the force was reasonable and not excessive is covered by ***s76/77 Criminal Justice and*** , and clarifies that a person acting for a legitimate purpose may not be able estimate the exact measure of necessary action. In this scenario, the force could be seen as reasonable/excessive, [**give evidence from scenario**], as in ***Clegg/Martin***.
- Therefore, D would/would not be able to plead the defence of self-defence.

Continued

Intoxication

- D may be able to use the defence of intoxication due to [**give evidence from scenario**].
- Intoxication can be   or   . Voluntary intoxication is where D chose to take an intoxicating substance and involuntary intoxication is where D did not know they were taking an intoxicating substance, including taking prescription drugs that unexpectedly made them intoxicated. In this scenario, the intoxication can be seen to be voluntary/involuntary because [**give evidence from scenario**].
- Where D was voluntarily intoxicated and charged with a   intent offence, voluntary intoxication can negate any mens rea if D was so intoxicated they did not form the mens rea for the offence. Here, [**give evidence from scenario**], as in   ***and Moore***, where the Ds were too drunk to have formed the intent to cause GBH or murder and so were not guilty of murder. If D has formed the mens rea despite being intoxicated however, they are still guilty.
- Where D was voluntarily intoxicated and charged with a   intent offence, intoxication is not a defence under the ruling in   because D took a reckless course of conduct in getting intoxicated. This recklessness is the intent for a basic intent offence and so D cannot rely on this. Here, [**give evidence from scenario**].
- Where D was involuntarily intoxicated but had the necessary mens rea when committing the offence, they will be guilty, as shown in   . This is because D's intoxicated state has not impacted on their ability to form mens rea.

Words to use
Barnes
basic
Hussain
Immigration Act 2008
involuntary
Jones
Kingston
Majewski
necessary
prevention of crime
reasonable
Sheehan
specific
voluntary
Wilson

Activity 3.17 Insanity and automatism

Draw lines to match the cases to the correct facts.

***R v Clarke* (1972)**	Hardening of the arteries was within the rules of insanity as his condition affected his mental reasoning, memory and understanding.
***R v Kemp* (1956)**	A defendant who injured his girlfriend while he was asleep fell within the definition of insanity as it was an internal cause.
***R v Sullivan* (1984)**	A diabetic who failed to take his insulin fell within the definition of insanity.
***R v Hennessy* (1989)**	Mere absent mindedness or confusion is not insanity.
***R v Burgess* (1991)**	Defendant was suffering from a mental disorder and killed his wife, but admitted that he knew what he had done was legally wrong.
***R v Quick* (1973)**	A defendant who injured his friend during an epileptic fit was deemed insane as it included any organic or functional disease, even where it was temporary.
***R v Windle* (1952)**	A diabetic who failed to eat after taking his insulin was not insane as the cause was external.

Context

Consent is a defence that can be used in very limited circumstances to completely excuse a defendant from liability for non-fatal offences. It works by removing the unlawful aspect of the defendant's conduct so that no crime has been committed.

The defence of consent seeks to balance the right of the victim to agree to particular activities that may be harmful to them with the role of the state in protecting its citizens from danger.

Consent can only be pleaded successfully if it is genuine; that is, the victim understood what they were giving their consent to, and were old and mature enough to understand. There must usually be a public policy reason why the defendant and victim should be allowed to engage in such a harmful activity.

A person can consent to common assault, but not to ABH or greater harm, unless it comes within the established exceptions of:

- properly conducted games and sports
- tattooing
- body piercing
- horseplay
- dangerous exhibitions
- reasonable surgical interference. Consent is available for doctors, nurses, dentists etc. carrying out medical procedures (AG's ref). Otherwise whenever any procedure was performed they would risk prosecution.

Consent must be true and informed. **True consent** is where the victim understands the nature and quality of the activity they are agreeing to. **Informed consent** is where the victim makes a decision while fully aware of all the risks involved and with the capacity to do so.

Implied consent is where the victim is assumed to consent, for example to minor touching in everyday life.

Mistaken belief in consent is a defence based on an 'honest mistake' about whether or not the victim is consenting.

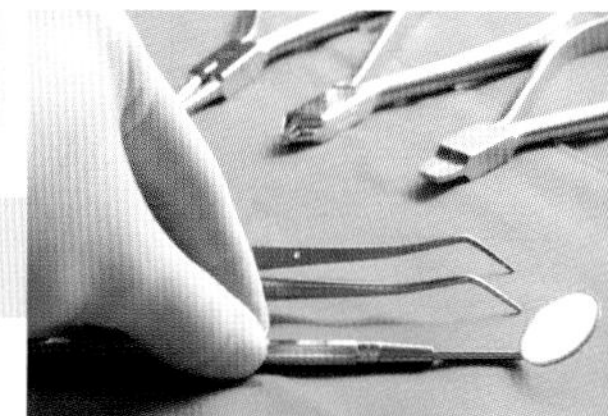

Activity 3.18 Consent

Research the cases and identify the facts and point of law.

Category	Case	Facts	Point of law
True consent	***Richardson (1999)***	Defendant was a dentist who continued to perform surgery even after being dismissed by her professional body.	Victims had only been deceived about her status as a practising dentist; the nature and quality of the acts performed were exactly those consented to, therefore, true consent.
True consent	***Tabassum (2000)***		
Informed consent	***Dica (2004)***		
Informed consent	***Gillick (1986)***		Provided the girl understood advice and the decisions she made were in her best interests, she was able to decide to use a contraceptive pill without her parents' input. Created a legal principle called Gillick competence.
Implied consent	***Collins v Wilcock (1984)***		By saying any touching, no matter how trivial, is battery, the court has to qualify this in some way with the use of implied consent (otherwise we would all be guilty of a crime).

Continued

Category	Case	Facts	Point of law
Mistaken belief in consent	***Jones (1986)***		
Mistaken belief in consent	***Aitkin (1992)***		
Mistaken belief in consent	***Richardson and Irwin (1999)***		
Properly conducted games and sports	***Barnes (2004)***		
Body art	***Wilson (1996)***		
Horseplay	***Jones (1986)***		

Context

Automatism is a complete defence and the defendant is not guilty if successful with a plea that their actions were involuntary and not consciously under their control. There is no voluntary actus reus and the defendant does not have the mens rea.

This may sometimes overlap with insanity when the defendant does not know the nature and quality of their actions (i.e. they do not know what they are doing).

- If the defendant is rendered an automaton by an internal factor, the insanity defence may apply under the M'Naghten rules.

- If defendant is rendered an automaton by an external factor, the automatism defence may apply under the Bratty rules, which define automatism as an act done by the muscles without any control by the mind, such as a spasm, a reflex action or a convulsion; or an act done by a person who is not conscious of what they are doing, such as while suffering from concussion or sleep-walking.
- 'Disease of the mind' is a legal and not a medical term. It has caused problems and is one of the reasons that the defence has come in for so much criticism. Because it is a legal definition, the judge can take into account policy in deciding which diseases are covered by M'Naghten.

Activity 3.19 Automatism case law

Research the cases and fill in the table to show how they have influenced how the law is applied.

Case	Facts	Decision/Point of law
1. The loss of control must be total		
Broome v Perkins (1987)		
Attorney-General's Reference 1992		
2. The cause of the automatism must be external		
Hill and Baxter (1958)	Defendant was in a collision and claimed he had been overcome by an unknown illness.	'A person should not be made liable at the criminal law who…'
R v T (1990)		

Continued

Case	Facts	Decision/Point of law
3. Self-induced automatism is a defence to specific but not basic intent crimes		
Bailey (1983)		
4. If defendant does not know their actions are likely to lead to an automatic state, they have not been reckless and can use automatism		
Hardie (1984)		

Activity 3.20 Automatism scenarios

Can the defendants rely on automatism as a defence? Refer to relevant cases in your answers.

1. Lucy is cycling home from work one day when a branch falls from a tree and hits her on the head. She is concussed and, rather than cycle down the road, ends up cycling inside a busy shop, causing damage to it.
Case:
Application:
2. John takes some sleeping pills to help him get a good night's sleep. He wakes in the morning on top of a neighbour's car. During the night he has scratched the car's bonnet with a key.
Case:
Application:
3. Anna is diabetic. While her blood-sugar level is out of balance, she crashes her car, damaging a street lamp.
Case:
Application:

Activity 3.21 Insanity key facts

Test yourself on the defence of insanity by answering these questions.

1. Insanity is a general defence. What does this mean?
2. What is the basic presumption applying to everyone?
3. Who has the burden of proving insanity on balance of probabilities?
4. Who else can raise the issue if evidence of the defendant's insanity is raised during the trial?
5. Be careful not to say that a person is convicted/guilty of insanity in your answers. What is the term for the correct verdict (also known as the special verdict)?
6. Which Act does this verdict come from?
7. What are the basic facts of the ***M'Naghten (1843)*** case?
8. What are the three key elements of the M'Naghten rules?
9. What does **defect of reason** mean?
10. What happened in the case of ***Clarke (1972)*** and why was her conviction quashed?

Activity 3.22 Disease of the mind

What do the following cases illustrate about the term 'disease of the mind'?

Kemp (1956)

Sullivan (1984)

Hennessy (1989)

Continued

Burgess (1991)

Activity 3.23 Self-defence and the Criminal Justice and Immigration Act 2008

Discuss the answers to these questions with someone else in your group.

1. Explain what the effect of ***subsections 3 and 4 Criminal Justice and Immigration Act 2008*** is on self-defence.
2. ***Section 76(4)(a)*** of the Act states that 'the reasonableness or otherwise of that belief is relevant to the question whether D genuinely held it'. What does this mean?
3. Can a person who has made a mistake because they are drunk or high on drugs rely on self-defence as a defence?
4. ***Section 76(6)*** says force shall not be regarded as 'reasonable in the circumstances ... if it was disproportionate in those circumstances'. What does this mean?
5. What allowances can be made, when deciding if the defendant has acted reasonably?

Activity 3.24 Self-defence, pre-emptive strike or excessive force?

Identify the cases that are described in the table.

Case	Facts	Ratio decidendi
	The defendant intervened in what he thought was a fight, saying he was a police officer trying to make an arrest. In fact, one person had just mugged a woman and the other was trying to arrest him. The defendant was prosecuted for assault.	The defendant had a genuine mistaken belief that may or may not have been reasonable.
	During riots, the defendant's shop was repeatedly targeted by looters. He stayed inside the shop overnight to prepare homemade petrol bombs.	It was held there is no obligation to wait until you are under an immediate threat. A pre-emptive strike is permitted as part of self-defence.
	A soldier on checkpoint duty during the conflict in Northern Ireland tried to stop a car but shot and killed a passenger as it sped off.	The defendant's final shot, which killed the person, was fired when the car was no longer a threat. Use of lethal force was therefore excessive in the circumstances.
	The defendant lived on an isolated farm prone to burglaries. He was woken in the night by people breaking in and shot them as they ran away.	On the basis that the burglars were fleeing the crime scene, they were no longer a direct threat and therefore use of the gun was excessive.

3.3 Quickfire questions

1. What are the M'Naghten rules?
2. What is the difference between the decisions in ***R v Quick*** and ***R v Hennessy***?
3. What is meant by **self-induced automatism**?
4. Why is intoxication not a true defence?
5. What are the three situations in which self-defence can be used?
6. What are the differences between the defences of duress by threats and duress of circumstances?
7. How was the defence of duress of circumstances extended in ***R v Martin (1989)***?
8. How do the courts decide whether it was necessary to use force in self-defence and whether it was reasonable to do so?
9. A disease of the mind must be caused by what type of factor for the defence of insanity?
10. What is the Graham test and why was it introduced?

Glossary

actus reus: 'the guilty act', an act, an omission or state of affairs that is the voluntary prohibited conduct.

breach of contract: to break a contract by not following its terms and conditions.

bundle of rights: the owner of a property has a bundle of rights over their own property, so they have the right to do anything with it (e.g. destroy it, throw it away or do something random with it).

claimant: the person bringing the action. Until April 1999, this person was called the plaintiff.

common law (also **case law** or **precedent):** law developed by judges through decisions in court.

constructive manslaughter: the death of a person is caused by an unlawful and dangerous criminal act.

damages: an award of money that aims to compensate the innocent party for the financial losses they have suffered as a result of the breach.

defendant: the person defending the action (e.g. the person accused of a crime).

equitable: fair.

exclusion clause: an attempt by one party to a contract to exclude all liability or to limit liability for breaches of the contract.

express terms: contract terms laid down by the parties themselves.

foreseeable: events the defendant should be able to have predicted could happen.

gross negligence manslaughter: the death of a person caused by civil negligence.

held: decided; the decision of the court.

homicide: the killing of one person by another, deliberately or not.

implied terms: contract terms that are assumed, either by common law or statute.

indictable: the most serious offences, triable only in the Crown Court.

intangible property: property that does not physically exist, such as copyright or patents.

maliciously: interpreted as meaning with intention or subjective recklessness.

mens rea: the mental element, the 'guilty mind',or the fault element of the offence.

objective: a test that considers not the defendant in question, but what another average, reasonable person would have done or thought if placed in the same position as the defendant.

real property: land and buildings.

remedy: an award made by a court to the innocent party in a civil case to 'right the wrong'.

representation: a statement made during contract negotiations that is not intended to be a part of the contract.

rescission: to unmake a contract or transaction, to return the parties to the position they would be in if it had never happened.

special defence: the use of a defence which has the effect not of completely acquitting the defendant but allowing a reduction in the sentence given to the defendant.

statute (Act of Parliament): a source of primary legislation that comes from the UK legislature.

strict liability: crimes where the prosecution does not have to prove mens rea against the defendant.

subjective: an assumption relating to the individual in question (the subject).

suicide pact: a partial defence to murder contained in ***s4 Homicide Act 1957*** whereby, if a surviving person of a pact for two people to die can prove that they both intended to die, the charge will be reduced to voluntary manslaughter.

term: a statement made during contract negotiations that is intended to be a part of the contract, binding the parties to it.

thing (or chose) in action: property that does not exist in a physical sense but which provides the owner with legally enforceable rights (e.g. a bank account, investments, shares and intellectual property such as patents).

tort: a civil wrong committed by one individual against another, such as injury caused by negligence.

triable either way: an offence that can be tried in either a magistrates' court or in the Crown Court.

vicarious liability: in the civil law of tort, a third party (e.g. an employer) can be held responsible for a tort committed by another (e.g. an employee).

***vis major*:** Latin for 'a superior force'. Used in civil cases to denote an act of God or loss resulting from natural causes, such as a hurricane, tornado, or earthquake, and without the intervention of human beings.

Index

Photo acknowledgements

p.4 Chinnapong / Shutterstock.com; p.10 Tyler Olsen / Shutterstock.com; p.11 Chinnapong / Shutterstock.com; p.13 (top) astarot / Shutterstock.com; p.13 (bottom) Preechar Bowonkitwancha / Shutterstock.com; p.14 (top) Tepikina Nastya / Shutterstock.com; p.14 (bottom) INDz / Shutterstock.com; p.19 Avigator Fortuner / Shutterstock.com; p.20 fizkes / Shutterstock.com; p.21 (top) Nomad_Soul / Shutterstock.com; p.21 (bottom) MaraZe / Shutterstock.com; p.22 Guschenkova / Shutterstock.com; p.23 (top) Sashkin / Shutterstock.com; p.23 (bottom) Matt Jones / Shutterstock.com; p.24 nd3000 / Shutterstock.com; p.26 mooremedia / Shutterstock.com; p.27 4Max / Shutterstock.com; p.28 JamesChen / Shutterstock.com; p.29 pathdoc / Shutterstock.com; p.30 (top) Witthaya IOvE / Shutterstock.com; p.30 (bottom) MicroOne / Shutterstock.com; p.31 Cherries / Shutterstock.com; p.32 sandyman / Shutterstock.com; p.33 Joe Gough / Shutterstock.com; p.34 I Love Coffee dot Today / Shutterstock.com; p.35 puhhha / Shutterstock.com; p.36 Silatip / Shutterstock.com; p.37 William Perugini / Shutterstock.com; p.38 Pormezz / Shutterstock.com; p.39 Paolo Bona / Shutterstock.com; p.40 mountainpix / Shutterstock.com; p.41 (top) PabloBenii / Shutterstock.com; p.41 (bottom) Vasyl Shuga / Shutterstock.com; p.42 Liukov / Shutterstock.com; p.44 sfam_photo / Shutterstock.com; p.45 Praisaeng / Shutterstock.com; p.46 (top) Brian A Jackson / Shutterstock.com; p.46 (bottom) Africa Studio / Shutterstock.com; p.48 punghi / Shutterstock.com; p.49 Billion Photos / Shutterstock.com; p.50 Aloneontheroad / Shutterstock.com; p.51 Brian A Jackson / Shutterstock.com; p.52 Radu Bercan / Shutterstock.com; p.53 Alexander Kirch / Shutterstock.com; p.55 (top) Photographee.eu / Shutterstock.com; p.55 (bottom) DDekk / Shutterstock.com; p.56 akatiev / Shutterstock.com; p.57 ChaiyonS021 / Shutterstock.com; p.58 ThamKC / Shutterstock.com; p.59 Iakov Filimonov / Shutterstock.com; p.62 Brian A Jackson / Shutterstock.com; p.63 Brian A Jackson / Shutterstock.com; p.65 baranq / Shutterstock.com; p.66 Mike_shots / Shutterstock.com; p.68 Syda Productions / Shutterstock.com; p.70 Zinenko Elena / Shutterstock.com; p.71 Pkpix / Shutterstock.com; p.72 wavebreakmedia / Shutterstock.com; p.73 antoniodiaz / Shutterstock.com; p.75 Miinam / Shutterstock.com; p.77 Africa Studio / Shutterstock.com; p.78 SofiaV / Shutterstock.com; p.80 PopTika / Shutterstock.com